Implementing the Common Core State Standards through Mathematical Problem Solving

Kindergarten– Grade 2

Sydney L. Schwartz
Queens College of the City University of New York

Frances R. Curcio, Series Editor
Queens College of the City University of New York

NCTM®

NATIONAL COUNCIL OF
TEACHERS OF MATHEMATICS

ISBN: 978-0-87353-723-0

The Cataloging-in-Publication Data is on file
with the Library of Congress.

The National Council of Teachers of Mathematics is the public voice of mathematics education, supporting teachers to ensure equitable mathematics learning of the highest quality for all students through vision, leadership, professional development, and research.

Printed in the United States of America

Contents

Series Editor's Foreword

The purpose of *Implementing the Common Core State Standards through Mathematical Problem Solving: Kindergarten–Grade 2*, as well as of the other books in the series (those for grades 3–5, grades 6–8, and high school), is to (1) provide examples of how instruction that focuses on developing mathematical problem-solving skills supports the Common Core State Standards (CCSS), (2) help teachers interpret the standards in ways that are useful for practice, and (3) provide examples of rich mathematical tasks and ways of implementing them in the classroom that have specific links to multiple standards. The books in this series are not meant to be comprehensive collections of mathematics problems for the entire school curriculum; instead, they contain rich problems and tasks in selected topics designed to develop several mathematics concepts and presented in ways that illustrate the connections and interrelatedness between CCSS and mathematical problem solving.

The Common Core State Standards for Mathematics

In June 2010, responding to the declining achievement of United States schoolchildren in reading and mathematics both nationally and when compared internationally, the National Governors Association and the Council for Chief State School Officers (NGA Center and CCSSO) issued the *Common Core State Standards* (http://www.corestandards.org). The CCSS program is an effort to provide a unified, national effort to strengthen the ability of future citizens to be globally competitive, while preparing them for college and career readiness. The standards and practices across the grades are expectations for improving the teaching and learning of mathematics. Toward this concerted effort, a large majority of the states, along with the Washington, D.C., school system, have adopted CCSS.

Similar to the standards in *Principles and Standards for School Mathematics* (National Council of Teachers of Mathematics 2000), the essential content in the Common Core State Standards for Mathematics (CCSSM) is included in several content areas ("domains") with various degrees of specificity: Counting and Cardinality, Operations and Algebraic Thinking, Number and Operations in Base Ten, Measurement and Data, and Geometry, with modeling expected to be integrated throughout the other content areas. An overview of the CCSSM standards for mathematics in kindergarten through grade 5 is included in appendix 1.

For each content area and grade level, the eight Standards for Mathematical Practice, which may be considered as fundamental elements of mathematical problem solving, are stated as follows:

CCSS Standards for Mathematical Practice

MP.1	Make sense of problems and persevere in solving them.
MP.2	Reason abstractly and quantitatively.
MP.3	Construct viable arguments and critique the reasoning of others.
MP.4	Model with mathematics.
MP.5	Use appropriate tools strategically.
MP.6	Attend to precision.
MP.7	Look for and make use of structure.
MP.8	Look for and express regularity in repeated reasoning. (NGA Center and CCSSO 2010)

These practices are highlighted throughout the problem-solving tasks and activities contained in each of the books in this series.

Mathematical Problem Solving

Although problem solving has always been a goal of mathematics instruction, Pólya's helpful guide, *How to Solve It* (1957), had been in print for several decades before the publication of *An Agenda for Action* in 1980, in which the National Council of Teachers of Mathematics (NCTM) asserted the importance of mathematical problem solving in the school curriculum. That is, *"the mathematics curriculum should be organized around problem solving"* (NCTM 1980, p. 2, original in italics).

But what is mathematical problem solving? Throughout the years, although not research-based, instruction in developing mathematical problem-solving skills has relied on Pólya's (1957) four-step approach: understanding the problem, developing a plan, carrying out the plan, and looking back to determine whether the solution makes sense.

At the heart of the problem-solving process is determining what a problem consists of for learners of mathematics. Different from a familiar exercise or example for which learners have a prescribed approach for obtaining a solution, a "problem" is usually non-routine and nontraditional, and the learner needs to bring strategies, tools, and insights to bear in order to solve it (Henderson and Pingry 1953). In the late 1980s, textbooks and supplemental resource materials highlighted various problem-solving strategies to assist learners in approaching and solving problems. Such strategies as guessing and checking, using a drawing, making a table or an organized list, finding a pattern, using logical reasoning, solving a simpler problem, and working backward (O'Daffer 1988) became staples of mathematics instruction.

Much of the research on mathematical problem solving was conducted in the mid-1970s through the late 1980s (Schoenfeld 2007). The intent was not to focus on solving a given problem but rather on examining how to help learners develop strategies to tackle problems and real-world applications. Throughout the years, as attempts have been made to concentrate and manage the complexity of studying various aspects of mathematical problem solving, research attention has been redirected to mathematical modeling (Lesh and Zawojewski 2007; Lester and Kehle 2003). According to Henry Pollak:

> Problem solving may not refer to the outside world at all. Even when it does, problem solving usually begins with the idealized real-world situation in mathematical terms, and ends with a mathematical result. Mathematical modeling, on the other hand, begins in the "unedited" real world, requires problem formulating before problem solving, and once the problem is solved, moves back into the real world where the results are considered in their original context. (Pollak 2011)

The Common Core State Standards suggest that instruction in mathematics integrate modeling in mathematical tasks and activities, and they identify specific standards for which modeling is recommended, thus challenging teachers, curriculum developers, and textbook authors to bring authentic, real-world data into the classroom. Through mathematical problem solving and modeling, students' experience in mathematics will extend beyond traditional, routine word problems.

With its Essential Understanding (NCTM 2010–13) and Focus in High School Mathematics: Reasoning and Sense Making (NCTM 2009–10) series, NCTM has offered ideas to help teachers actively involve students in analyzing and solving problems. The Implementing the Common Core State Standards through Mathematical Problem Solving series contributes to these efforts, specifically supporting the connections between CCSS and mathematical problem solving.

The author of this book, Sydney L. Schwartz, is gratefully acknowledged for sharing her insights and ideas to help early primary grade teachers meet the challenges of implementing the CCSS. Thanks are due to the NCTM Educational Materials Committee for making the development of this manuscript possible, and to Joanne Hodges, director of publications; Myrna Jacobs, publications manager; and the NCTM publications staff for their guidance, advice, and technical support in the preparation of the manuscript.

Frances R. Curcio
Series Editor

Preface

The mathematics curriculum in kindergarten through grade 2 provides many rich opportunities for children to learn and do mathematics through problem solving. Hands-on, minds-on, appropriate experiential activities pique children's interests and curiosity, and they contribute to building mathematical problem-solving skills and strategies. As stated in *Principles and Standards for School Mathematics:* "Problem solving in the early years should involve a variety of contexts, from problems related to daily routines to mathematical situations arising from stories" (National Council of Teachers of Mathematics 2000, p. 116). The six different contexts described in chapter 1 provide the settings for the tasks presented in each of the chapters that follow it.

Building on NCTM recommendations (NCTM 2011), the Common Core State Standards for Mathematics (CCSSM) further develop the standards for how children go about doing mathematics, and thus include standards for "mathematical practice" in addition to standards for "mathematical content." Teachers have the new challenge of maintaining an environment conducive to problem solving in their classrooms while meeting the requirements of the CCSSM.

The purpose of this book is to guide teachers in kindergarten through grade 2 in their efforts to implement these standards, both for mathematical content and for mathematical practice. As the title suggests, the emphasis here is on meeting the standards through a problem-solving approach, not only as a means of practicing what has been learned but also as a tool to "build new mathematical knowledge" (NCTM 2000, p. 52).

This book contains a total of nineteen problems, identified here as "tasks," some of which include variations and extensions. These tasks are organized by grade level within the following chapters: Number, Computation, and Algebra; Geometry; and Measurement and Data. Modeling does not have its own chapter, because it is incorporated within each task. Each of these tasks is related to a specific domain and cluster of standards within the Common Core. Examples of student-teacher interactions are provided to illustrate how to develop mathematical problem-solving skills and support the Common Core Standards.

The collection of tasks in this book is not meant to be a complete curriculum. These tasks are designed to highlight engaging ways to involve children in exploring mathematical relationships, and in modeling and expressing their ideas orally, in diagrams, in tables, and with manipulative materials. Not every CCSSM domain and cluster is represented, and only interesting problems that lend themselves to meaningful implementation of content standards have been included. Where appropriate, the Standards for Mathematical Practice that best meet the intent of the problem are discussed. Depending on teachers' knowledge of their students, tasks may be modified to meet children's needs.

This book is intended for use by teachers in kindergarten through grade 2, providing a source of rich problems to develop early mathematical concepts as well as to exemplify mathematics learning through problem solving. Teacher educators may use this book as a supplemental text in a mathematics methods course for primary grade teachers or in a curriculum course for preservice teachers. This would help preservice teachers become increasingly familiar with the Common Core State Standards for Mathematics and how they may be implemented. Readers should find the CCSS Overview for Mathematics in Kindergarten through Grade 5 in appendix 1 helpful in providing a "vertical" overview of the major content areas and how they are emphasized through the elementary grades. Finally, the two-dimensional and three-dimensional diagrams and vocabulary for geometric shapes in appendix 2 may serve as a resource for naming and discussing geometric shapes.

Chapter 1
Contexts for Promoting Problem Solving

Mathematics is a participant sport. Children must play it frequently to become good at it.
(National Research Council 2009, p. 125)

Our primary goal in mathematics education is to empower young children as problem solvers using mathematical understandings and skills featured in the Common Core State Standards for Mathematics (CCSSM). In order for children to achieve fluency as problem solvers, we need to expose them to multiple problem-solving strategies in different contexts that capture and sustain their interest and help them to reflect on the problem-solving process (National Research Council 2009).

From the ages of five to eight, children move through a significant period of cognitive growth. They increasingly make connections between what they have learned through experiences with materials in the concrete world and what they are learning through problems that require mathematical understandings and skills. Their early mathematical knowledge is directly linked to physical knowledge—that is, knowledge about the properties of objects gained through the senses (Rowan and Bourne 2001). Throughout these years, the balance shifts from learning based on discovering relationships between objects and actions through "hands-on" activities to learning through experiences of applying knowledge based on prior understandings. Children have an increasingly larger well of stored experiences, and this serves as the reservoir for mentally constructing answers to problems involving number, geometry, and measurement. However, the validation of solutions continues to require the use of real-world props, which in turn stimulates interest in learning more.

The major contexts that activate problem solving using mathematics in this developmental period occur during experiences in which children are doing the following:

1. Discovering mathematical content and relationships propelled by their own interests;
2. Organizing ongoing activities and planning activity sequences for materials management and scheduling purposes;
3. Engaging in playful activities and games organized by peers and adults;
4. Constructing products using art, craft, and other concrete materials;

5. Satisfying curiosity to solve a mathematical problem or figure out a mathematical relationship; and

6. Pursuing integrated curriculum activities in the form of topical studies, projects, and those activities related to literature.

The first five contexts are ones that permeate children's lives before they enter school. They serve as guidelines for designing curriculum activities that will engage and sustain children's interests in expanding mathematical knowledge that extends their problem-solving abilities. The last context is one that typically occurs in school.

CONTEXT 1—*Discovering mathematical content and relationships propelled by their own interests*

During the preprimary years, children are continually manipulating the rich variety of materials in their environment. For example, they count the peas on their plate, or they line them up or arrange them in a circle. Either deliberately or unintentionally, adults frequently use mathematical strategies related to measurement and number to facilitate daily events (e.g. "Do you want the bigger apple or a smaller one?" or "Just five more minutes, and we'll go to the park."). As children take on more responsibility for organizing their actions, they increase their awareness of number, geometry, and measurement relationships. Similarly, as they play with more of the objects that surround them, they not only compare and contrast the properties of these things, but they group them for different purposes. While research has documented that children learn a great deal from play, as they enter the formal schooling years "it appears that they can learn much more with artful guidance and challenging activities provided by the teachers" (Seo and Ginsberg 2004, p. 103). By the time children enter kindergarten, they have accumulated a wealth of experience that involves quantitative and geometric thinking, although they may not be able to communicate the degree of their understandings (Sophian 1999).

The instructional challenge with children at this developmental stage is to "capture them thinking mathematics" so that, as they pursue their own interests, their intuitive thinking is brought to the conscious level. The teacher's role here is to help children make a connection between the informal, intuitive mathematics and formal, school mathematics (Copley 2010). This is achieved by initiating conversation based on the adult observations. For example, if the child is pasting shapes to create a clown's face, an observational comment that translates action into words might be, "I noticed that you picked up a triangle to paste on the clown's face as the second eye and then decided to use a circle instead. Is that because the first eye was a circle?" Then, as the child continues by starting to take a circle and then selecting a triangle for the nose, the next question can focus on the child's decision: "I noticed that you were thinking about the circle or the triangle for the nose. Is there a special reason you chose a triangle for the nose instead of a circle?" In this instance, the child posed the problem and the adult invited an explanation of the solution (Schwartz and Copeland 2010). The kindergarten activity in chapter 3, which involves working with children in constructing with blocks, illustrates this context.

CONTEXT 2—*Organizing ongoing activities and planning activity sequences for materials management and scheduling purposes*

Children spontaneously plan many of their daily activities. For example, when several children are playing with a new set of materials, they distribute the items (i.e., *partitioning sets*) or place them in a central location accessible to everybody (i.e., *positioning a set*). When playing ball, they decide who goes first and who goes next in taking turns (i.e., *ordinal position and sequence*). Observing children as they pursue activities of their own choosing reveals how often they use mathematics to organize their use of materials. They show us in many ways how they use mathematical understandings and skills to control and anticipate their experiences.

In school, the need to solve problems using mathematics arises in planning and posting daily, weekly, and monthly schedules (i.e., *time measurement*); assigning classroom responsibilities and rotation of these responsibilities (i.e., *recording data*); and logging critical information for obtaining resources for such activities as snack and lunch (i.e., *number and computation*). Each of these activities serves a management purpose that creates opportunities for children to participate in solving time, space, number, and measurement problems in order to facilitate program activities. The two tasks for grade 1 found in chapter 4—planning a class trip and creating a calendar—involve children in this context.

CONTEXT 3—*Engaging in playful activities and games organized by peers and adults*

Playful activities designed and guided by the adult—such as copying and extending patterns with materials, following a musical beat with actions, or matching sets of objects in a mixed collection—may narrow the child's choices of how to use the materials or respond. But they can still retain the "high interest factor" associated with self-directed activities. These kinds of activities provide opportunities to increase the child's ability to identify mathematical relationships, and they feature problem solving in a given situation (e.g., inviting the child to justify the extension he has made to a bead pattern).

Similarly, playing games in which the player has to make some decisions narrows the choice of actions while simultaneously posing problems to be solved within the game structure (Eston and Economopoulos 1997; Kamii and DeVries 1980). Typical examples are a treasure hunt in which the players must figure out the meaning of locational and directional clues, a number game in which players must decide which numbers on their board to cover in order to make an equivalent match to the cue number, or a track game with alternative routes players may choose from to move to the end of the path. "In playing games, students tend to develop feelings of effectiveness and control because the actions they take in the game produce results" (Gordon 1972). The results of these choices contribute to the players' understandings of the mathematical relationships.

The adult role in this context includes:

- Designing games with increasing complexity so that the actions embedded in the game clearly focus on problem solving related to selected mathematical standards (Schwartz 2005).

- Observing the play of the game in order to collect information on the strategies the players are using to solve problems occurring during the play of the game for later discussion.

- Debriefing with the players about the problems they solved, in order to contribute to the players' thinking about the strategies they used.

Very simple games that offer no choices to the player, such as matching identical shapes with lotto cards or moving a specified number of spaces on a game board track, may be valuable tools for practicing mathematical skills, but they offer little opportunity to engage in mathematical problem solving. The adult role rests in the designing of the game and the debriefing with the players about the choices they made (Schwartz 2005).

Examples of tasks that fit within this context of playful activities include the kindergarten card games in chapter 2, the geometry game for grade 1 in chapter 3, and the kindergarten activity of matching lengths in chapter 4.

CONTEXT 4—*Constructing products using art, craft, and other concrete materials*

Making a product provides one of the richest opportunities for using mathematics to solve problems. Children quantify as they create, and they get immediate feedback on the success of their solution (Schirrmacher 1993). However, in order to realize this potential, children need opportunities for making choices that lead to thinking about problem solutions.

If a task is assigned (e.g., to make a three-dimensional model of the classroom), and the choice of materials is open, the problems posed involve selecting or making appropriately sized and shaped materials that can represent the objects in the classroom. This exercise also requires decisions about positioning the objects in the model at the right location and distance (Mitchell 1971; Sobel 1998). If, in contrast, the materials are assigned (e.g., precut paper shapes of different sizes and a collection of buttons, or a set of line stampers), the problems posed deal with selecting the goal of a product that can be created with the materials. In both approaches—either restricting the choice of product or restricting the choice of materials—the problems to be solved in producing a product involve linear measurement, joining shapes, and number (Barnett and Halls 2008; Lowenfeld 1958; Richardson 1964; Topal 2005).

For the least experienced learners, producing products with art, craft, and construction materials center more on discovering mathematical relationships than on applying knowledge to solve problems. The teacher's role here features helping children become aware of the mathematical relationships they are uncovering by sharing observations and extending conversations (e.g., "How did you decide on the size of the ears on this rabbit?").

For the more experienced learners, the decisions they make about what they want to produce provokes a greater need to use strategies to achieve their goal. Under these circumstances, the teaching role serves to help children to reflect on the strategies they used to solve problems and to think about alternative strategies (e.g., "How come you changed from using the string to using the wire when you were making the wheel for your car?").

The grade 2 activity in chapter 3, constructing three-dimensional objects from two-dimensional shapes, illustrates this context.

CONTEXT 5—*Being driven by curiosity to solve a mathematical problem or figure out a mathematical relationship*

It is not uncommon for a child or small group of children to become fascinated with exploring some mathematical relationship, such as figuring out how many ways they can match the weight of a specific object on a balance scale given objects of identical weights or several weights in ratio (Curcio and Schwartz 1997). The search serves no purpose other than to satisfy their curiosity. The inquiry may emerge spontaneously or be provoked by an adult who "wonders out loud" about a specific mathematical relationship related to an ongoing or recent curriculum activity.

The teacher role in this case rests primarily in setting up an investigation involving mathematical problem solving that captures the children's interests, and in focusing children's thinking on the mathematical strategies they are using to satisfy their curiosity.

The estimating tasks in the grade 2 section of chapter 2 offer an example of an activity driven by curiosity with significant mathematical possibilities. The grade 2 activity in chapter 4, measuring the power of magnets, also fits this context.

CONTEXT 6—*Pursuing integrated curriculum activities involving topical studies, projects, and literature*

Integrated curriculum activities, with their broad scope, present the most challenging contexts for focusing on problem solving using mathematical understandings. The many options make it essential to carefully plan in order to focus on identifying and solving problems that serve a purpose in the task while also featuring mathematical knowledge and skills related to the Common Core standards. For example, when studying growth and change in plants beginning with sprouting seeds, the most important embedded mathematical understanding relates to measurement. To support this learning, the adult needs to provide choices of measuring tools so that the children can solve the problem of which tool to use to measure the changes they observe as the seed matures into a seedling and then into a plant. The task of setting up a way to keep track of the changes associated with the various events they are observing provokes another kind of problem solving (e.g., how to record time intervals, change in size, appearance of leaves and their location on the plant). Both students and teachers need to participate in making decisions about what to measure and how to measure. In this type of activity, the role of the teacher involves helping students make choices of when, where, and how to use mathematical content to support the study of the topic.

When integrated curriculum activities take shape in projects, topics, and literature experiences, standards from all curriculum areas are naturally addressed, although not necessarily in each event that occurs as the project develops. One example would be if the theme is farm animals and the project is to build a model of a barn. In that case, life-science standards are addressed when identifying which farm animals need to be housed in the barn and what their needs are for care and feeding. Mathematics standards are addressed in the areas of measurement and number, as children figure out how many animals will be housed in the barn and the space each one needs. When using project activities to address standards, the broad scope of possibilities means the adult must carefully plan the choices offered to the children in order to create a focus on the use of mathematical strategies to achieve the goals in different segments of the project (Fromberg 2012; Helm and Katz 2011; Schwartz and Copeland 2010).

Similarly, the possibilities for pursuing a set of activities related to stories in literature have been extensively described in publications over the past two decades, as exemplified in the work of Whitin and Wilde (1992, 1995).

The grade 1 activities in chapter 2 on making mini-gardens illustrate several ways to make mathematics a central part of an integrated curriculum project.

Summary

The chapters that follow this introductory one deal with CCSSM K–2 standards and practices in the fields of number and operations, geometry, and measurement and data. All the tasks and activities presented in those fields are designed for engaging children in problem-solving situations and are framed in the six contexts identified above.

Kindergarten tasks feature activities that particularly capitalize on Context 1, *discovering mathematical content and relationships in activities propelled by children's own interests* (as in task 3.2, constructing with blocks), and on Context 3, *engaging in playful activities and games* (as in task 2.4, matching cards with pictured sets, and in tasks 4.1 and 4.2, comparing the length of wooden dowels).

Grade 1 tasks illustrate Context 2, *planning activity sequences and scheduling* (as in task 4.3, scheduling a class trip); Context 3, *engaging in playful activities and games* (as in task 3.4, playing a shape game); and Context 6, *pursuing an integrated curriculum activity* (as in task 2.5, a planting activity).

Grade 2 tasks focus on Context 4, *constructing products* (as in task 3.6, constructing a 3-D object from 2-D shapes), and on Context 5, *satisfying curiosity* (as in task 2.7, estimating quantities, and in task 4.5, measuring the power of magnets).

For all tasks and for all grades, the emphasis is on engaging and sustaining children's interest in using mathematical understandings to achieve a goal and to reflect on the strategies used to achieve it.

Chapter 2

Number, Computation, and Algebra

When students start to notice that mathematical situations have particular properties or a certain structure, they are beginning to think algebraically. (Johanning et al. 2009–10, p. 300)

W hen children are learning number, computation, and algebra, a primary goal is to engage them in activities that increase their ability to reason about quantities. Reasoning leads to recognizing patterns of numerical relationships, which in turn expands problem-solving capabilities. For example, the pattern in interval counting, often labeled *skip counting,* is the regularity of the numerical distance between the numbers in the sequence. In their spontaneous activities, children often show an awareness of the pattern of single alternation without number (e.g., when they step from one pavement block to the next, skipping each line that divides the blocks). As children gain experience in using number to quantify, they have many more opportunities to recognize patterns. They discover, for example, that when you share six cookies with one other person, you each get three cookies, but when there are seven cookies you have a problem to be solved. The following six key areas of early number sense and arithmetic are developmental, and they coincide with the kindergarten–grade 2 standards of the Common Core State Standards for Mathematics (CCSSM):

1. Using numbers to quantify collections;
2. Using numbers to compare collections;
3. Adding and subtracting single-digit numbers;
4. Understanding part-whole relations;
5. Equal partitioning or grouping for equivalency;
6. Grouping and place value. (Baroody 2004)

These areas of learning are not necessarily discrete. By the time children use number to quantify collections, they probably have already made informal comparisons of quantity. Therefore the counting overlaps and integrates with the comparison process. Similarly, children may spontaneously partition a collection into equal groups as part of the process of building understandings about part-whole relations. Consequently, when designing activities to strengthen young children's ability to apply understandings in problem-solving situations, the focus on these areas will overlap.

The number and algebra standards for kindergarten–grade 2 are partitioned into three domains. The first domain, Counting and Cardinality, is specified for kindergarten only. The next two domains, Operations and Algebraic Thinking along with Number and

Operations, embrace all three grade levels, with a focus for grades 1 and 2 on base ten. These standards define the sequence for understanding the relationship between addition and subtraction, understanding place value, and working with equivalent groups of objects to gain a foundation for multiplication in grades 1 and 2.

What follows are tasks presented according to grade levels. The kindergarten tasks in this chapter focus on solving problems through the process of quantifying and matching sets for equivalency (as in task 2.1), identifying intervals of 2 in the counting sequence 1 to 10 (task 2.2), solving simple addition problems using the numbers 1 to 9 (task 2.3), and matching numerals to sets (task 2.4). The tasks take place in the context of playful activities and games as children use one set of materials. For grade 1, the related tasks 2.5 and 2.6 feature addition and subtraction up to 100 in the context of an integrated curriculum activity. For grade 2, tasks 2.7 and 2.8 come with multiple variations, including one- and two-step problems that involve addition and subtraction in the context of satisfying student curiosity.

The eight Standards for Mathematical Practice (MP), as listed on page vi, are woven throughout the domains. Depending on the problem, the relevant Standards (identified as, for example, "MP.3") are discussed after the description of the task.

Kindergarten

The ability to subitize—that is, to "recognizing the numerosity of a group quickly" without counting (Copley 2010, p. 54)—increases with multiple experiences in high-interest activities. Young children enjoy activities in which the goal is to accumulate more items (increasing the set size) or instead to eliminate the items, and these activities provide multiple opportunities to repeatedly quantify sets and "count to tell the number of objects" of different numerical quantities (National Governors Association Center for Best Practices and Council of Chief State School Officers 2010, p. 11). The following tasks 2.1 through 2.4 address the cluster of standards in counting and cardinality for kindergarten. They begin with simple counting to match sets for equivalency and then progress to comparing quantity and doing simple addition.

Task 2.1

Task summary: Create a deck of playing cards with pictured sets of 1 through 10 by pasting precut shapes or pictures on 3×4-inch cards representing quantities 1 through 10. Use the cards in an activity of matching for equivalency.

Materials:

- Blank 3×4-inch cards
- Precut shapes for pasting
- Paste
- Crayons or markers
- Lined paper for each child for recording the pairs of cards accumulated

Step 1—*Invite the children to use the precut materials to create a deck of 20 cards, with two cards representing each of the numbers 1 through 10.* After the children complete the task, have them verify that they now have the correct number of cards, two for each number of 1 through 10. Engage them in comparing their cards with those of their peers, and have them discuss what they notice about the different ways the sets are arranged. As the children point to the arrangements of items on the cards and use their own language to describe them, introduce the labels used to describe the different patterns. (Such descriptions include *linear* or *in a line; circular* or *in a circle; symmetrical* or *balanced;* and *random* or *without any special arrangement*). Wonder out loud which arrangements are the easiest to recognize and which ones they had to check by counting and recounting.

Step 2—*Explain and demonstrate an activity that requires matching two cards for equivalency.* First, assign partners, and designate one student in each pair as "Player 1" and the other as "Player 2." Ask the children to mix up their sets of cards so they are in an unpredictable order, and then stack them and place the stack face down on the table directly in front of where they are sitting with their partner. Direct the players to draw a card from their own stack. If the cards are equivalent, Player 1 keeps both cards, and if they are not equivalent, Player 2 keeps the cards. Players repeat this action until all the cards are used. At the end of the round, players count how many pairs of cards they have collected.

In order to avoid the typical "win-lose" competition, raise the question, "If you do this activity again, and you switch the roles of who gets the cards when they are equivalent and not equivalent, do you suppose you will have more or fewer pairs?" Suggest that the children begin a record of how many pairs they have accumulated. Repeat the activity several times and invite them to look at their record and talk about what they notice (for example, how many times they got the same number of pairs).

Step 3—*Discuss mathematical reflections.* Recall for the students the earlier discussion about which arrangements of sets on the cards were hardest to recognize and raise the question as to whether their opinion on this question has changed. Expand the discussion to brainstorm ways to rearrange the "hard to count" pictured sets to make it easier to recognize their quantities without counting (e.g., patterns that lead to the use of interval counting, by 2s, by 3s, by 4s, or by 5s). Invite the children to make a few more cards that conform with these new ideas, add the cards to the decks, and repeat the activity.

Task 2.2

Task summary: Identify an interval of 2 when matching quantities between 1 and 10.
Materials:

- The playing cards with sets of 1 through 10 that were made in task 2.1
- Lined paper for each child for recording the pairs of numbers accumulated
- Pencils or crayons

For this task, you will change the goal of using the playing cards to identify the numerical intervals in the size of the groups. For example, if the two drawn cards represent an interval of 2 (e.g., 4 and 6), Player 1 keeps the cards. If not, then Player 2 keeps them. After partners complete the activity for the first time, talk with them about how they figured out the interval between the numbers. Enrich the conversation by sharing observations of the strategies they used: "I noticed that Sam used his fingers to figure out the interval and that Natalie tapped her hand on the desk as she was counting." Summarize the different ways the children used to identify the interval.

Repeat the activity and ask the children to keep a record of the pairs of cards they collected for reference. Tell them to list the pairs with intervals of 2 (e.g., 2 and 4; 5 and 7) and the pairs that were not intervals of 2 (e.g., 2 and 6; 5 and 9). After several rounds of play, initiate conversation about their record of paired cards. Have them look for duplicate matches, and talk about which pairs were harder to figure out, and whether they were the ones with intervals of 2 or those that were not intervals of 2.

Task 2.3

Task summary: Count and add numbers between 1 and 9.
Materials:

- The playing cards with sets of 1 through 10 that were made in task 2.1
- Lined paper for each child for recording the pairs of numbers accumulated
- Pencils or crayons

For this task, change the goal to simple addition. As one possible example, Player 1 keeps cards that add up to a quantity greater than 6, and Player 2 keeps cards that add up to a quantity less than 6. After the first round, ask the children again to record the number combinations they have collected so they can review them when all the cards are used. Review with them their record of the number combinations, talking about what they notice about those combinations that added up to greater than 6, and about those that added up to less than 6. For example, when the sum is less than 6, there are no numbers listed that are greater than 5.

When a pair disagrees on the results of adding the numbers represented on two cards, the adult can raise the question of how they can be certain of the addition result; in other words, how can they check their answer?

After several rounds of play, share some of your observations of the strategies the children used to solve the problems as a way to initiate a discussion. For example: "I noticed that Jason decided to count all the items pictured on both cards to find out how many. I heard Stella say, *I know that 2 and 2 is 4 and one more makes 5,* using what she knew about doubling numbers to add." Encourage them to talk about other strategies they used to add the numbers.

Task 2.4

Task summary: Match numerals to sets 1 to 10.
Materials:

- The playing cards with sets of 1 through 10 that were made in task 2.1
- Lined paper for each child for recording the pairs of numbers accumulated
- Pencils or crayons
- More blank 3×4-inch cards for creating numeral cards

Have the children each create one set of numeral cards for 1 through 10, and add them to each deck they are using. Advise them that now they can match numerals with picture cards of the same quantity or numerals with numerals. Repeat the matching activity.

As they pursue the activity, note the challenges the children are dealing with and observe the strategies they use to decide which numerals match pictured sets. Afterward, encourage them to talk about what they were thinking as they solved the problem of matching equivalent cards.

Invite children to brainstorm on other possible variations. As they come up with ideas, raise the question of how the idea will change the mathematical task. Some partners may choose to increase the quantities they are manipulating by adding cards with greater numbers or invent a subtraction goal instead of an addition goal. (For example, if the result of subtracting one quantity from another is greater than 5, one child keeps the pair of cards, and vice versa.) Encourage each team to select one of the ideas they have generated, try it out, keep a record of the pairs they accumulate, and share the results with their peers. As groups invent more options, the adult can challenge them to extend the options and ultimately address the standard of "find[ing] the number that makes 10 when added to a given number" (NGA Center and CCSSO 2010, p. 11), and keeping a record of the results.

DISCUSSION—*Tasks 2.1 through 2.4*

The above sequence of activities addresses all the counting goals listed in CCSSM under the domain of Counting and Cardinality for kindergarten. As the activities increase in complexity, the children successively engage in counting by ones to identify the number of objects, supporting Standard K.CC 5, and realize that that quantity is determined through the process of counting regardless of the arrangement of the items in the set. They compare numbers to identify the quantity of sets as greater than or less than and match sets to written numerals, addressing Standards K.CC 6 and 7. These tasks also address some of the standards found in the Operations and Algebraic Thinking domain. Through these activities, children ultimately develop fluency in adding and subtracting within 5 (K.OA 5) and in solving simple computation problems involving numbers 1 to 10 (K.OA 1).

Because these activities occur with children in pairs, the level of the mathematical challenge can be adjusted for each group in terms of their emerging skills and understandings. Exposure to different learning levels can occur during group sharing sessions.

These activities also incorporate several of the Standards for Mathematical Practice listed on page vi. The problem-posing that is built into the tasks allows the teacher to encourage children to explain their thinking when disagreements arise (MP.3) and to attend to precision (MP.6).

Grade 1

The following activities for grade 1 build on the initial mastery of counting, comparing numbers, and simple computation as they address the standards related to number and operations in base 10. They are designed to take place in the context of an integrated curriculum activity. In tasks 2.5 and 2.6, students will develop the understanding that addition and subtraction are inverse operations. They will accomplish this goal through situations where numbers are added together for a purpose and the results of the addition computation are followed by undoing the action with repeated subtraction.

The occasion for this curriculum project can be selected by considering the geographical location of the school, the holidays usually celebrated in the community, and the interests of the class. For example, depending on the climate and the time of year, it might be a celebration of spring or the starting of a school garden. It also can serve program planning in communities where it is traditional to make gifts for parents on Mother's Day, Father's Day, or Grandparents' Day. The activity given here involves each child in planting a mini-garden with a selection of 5 seeds. It should be preceded by a project in which they have studied the way seeds sprout and the differences in sprouting time for different seeds (Chalufour and Worth 2003; Charlesworth and Lind 2010; Martin 2001).

Task 2.5

Task summary: Figure out the number of seed packets needed for a class planting project.
Materials:

- Chart paper and writing tools
- Planting containers and soil
- Three varieties of seeds
- Access to water

Step 1—*Pose the task of making individual mini-gardens with 5 seeds each using marigold, zinnia, and sweet alyssum seeds.* Review prior experiences in which children may have studied the sprouting of different kinds of seeds. Ask the students to think about how many seeds of each variety they want to plant. They should enter that information in a table that will be used to compute the total number of each type of seed needed for the class project (see table 2.1 for an example).

Table 2.1
Planning for mini-gardens

Name	Marigold	Zinnia	Sweet Alyssum
Matthew	2	2	1
Samantha	1	3	1
Charles	5	0	0
Total			

Ask the children to work in teams of two to compute the total number of seeds needed by the class for each variety. Invite them to compare the results of their computations and to share the strategies they used (e.g., counting all, clustering the equivalent numbers and then counting each cluster, or using familiar number facts). When they agree on the sums, help them reflect on the fact that no matter how they organized the numbers to be added together, the result was the same. Raise the question, "How many seeds do we need to buy altogether if we have 20 children in this class who have each chosen 5 seeds to plant?" Ask small groups of children to verify that the total number of seeds, including all three columns, correlates with the number of children in the class requesting 5 seeds each. Repeat the discussion of how they figured it out (e.g., modeling the problem by entering tallies of the total number and separating them into groups of 5, or counting by 5s with written numerals or using objects such as fingers).

Step 2—*Figure out the number of seed packets needed.* Advise the students that you found out from a gardener friend that most seed packets for these three varieties of flowers contain 50 seeds. Ask teams of students to figure out and record how many seed packets the class will need for the each type of seed to complete the mini-gardens. With them, compare and contrast the different approaches the children used to figure out the number of packets to buy.

Advise the children that when the seeds are distributed, they will need to think about what to do with the unused leftover seeds. Ask them to figure out how many seeds will be left over. Show them how to use a table such as table 2.2 to write this information down for later reference.

Table 2.2
Unused seeds by variety

Number of packets bought	Seeds *minus* used seeds = Number unused
Marigold seeds (2 packets)	$100 - 70 = 30$
Zinnia seeds (1 packet)	$50 - 35 = 15$
Sweet alyssum seeds (1 packet)	$50 - 20 = 30$

Engage children in the plans for obtaining materials for the planting of the seeds. In addition to soil, seeds, and access to water, this activity requires a sufficient number of containers measuring approximately 8 inches in length, 4 inches deep, and 3 inches wide. Options include half-gallon milk cartons cut in half lengthwise, aluminum foil baking pans, and plastic containers.

Step 3—*Develop a plan for distributing seeds.* After purchasing the seed packets, assign teams to verify that each packet did in fact have the expected 50 seeds. Brainstorm with the children to develop a plan to distribute the seeds. Encourage the children to think about different ways to partition the sets of seeds (e.g., assigning teams to set up sets of 5 according to the list, or having each child take the number requested).

Step 4—*Plant the seeds.* As children prepare the mini-gardens by placing soil in containers, raise the question of how they intend to space the seeds. Encourage them to share their reasons for the spacing decisions.

An integrated curriculum activity such as task 2.5 allows for discussion of a variety of topics, including the measurement of space in locating the seeds in the planter, the measurement of time related to sprouting, and the measurement of change in the size of the sprouts. It is important to maintain focus on the targeted mathematical standards—in this case, addition and subtraction up to 100—and avoid initiating too many diverse mathematical discussions within the one event.

Task 2.6

Task summary: Figure out the number of additional mini-gardens that can be made with the unused seeds.

After the class has completed the primary task of making mini-gardens to take home, raise the problem of what to do with the unused seeds, using the figures gathered in their version of table 2.2. As the students consider the different possibilities, pose a problem of how many gardens can be made if 10 seeds are planted instead of 5 seeds. Have the children work with partners, asking some teams to figure out how many planters can be made with 5 seeds, and others how many can be done with 10 seeds. When the various groups have figured out how many 5- or 10-seed planters can be made, encourage sharing on how they determined their answers. Raise the question as to which problem was easier, figuring out the 10-seed planters or the 5-seed planters, and discuss why they think this is so. Take advantage of the opportunity to reflect on the ease of working with the different intervals of 5 and 10.

DISCUSSION—*Tasks 2.5 and 2.6*

These two integrated curriculum activities are designed to take place over several combined mathematics and science instructional periods. They address CCSSM in two of its domains for grade 1: Operations and Algebraic Thinking, and Number and Operations in Base 10. Through successive activities, the children "[r]epresent and solve problems involving addition and subtraction," apply properties of operations as strategies to add and subtract within 100, and "extend the counting sequence" (NGA Center and CCSSO 2010, p. 14). The children "develop, discuss, and use efficient, accurate, and generalizable methods to add within 100" (NGA Center and CCSSO 2010, p. 13) as they engage in figuring out how many seeds to buy and how to distribute them.

These activities also have some relevance for a third domain of CCSSM in grade 1, Measurement and Data. Recording mathematical information during an activity allows for interpreting data and completing computations resulting from a study of the data (1.MD 4). While data analysis is not listed as a standard for grade 1, collecting and recording data are integral to many activities that address the standards in number, geometry, and measurement (Curcio 2010).

Several of the Standards for Mathematical Practice are met in completing these tasks. Discussions of the number of seeds needed compared to the number acquired activate those practices related to persevering in solving problems (MP.1), constructing viable arguments (MP.3), modeling with mathematics (MP.4), and attending to precision (MP.6). Because accuracy in results affects the success of the activity, these tasks also highlight the importance of precision (MP.6). And in addition to its mathematical components, this set of integrated curriculum activities also meets life-science goals related to understanding germination of seeds and the sequence of changes that occur as seedlings grow and change into flowering plants.

Grade 2

The following activities for grade 2—tasks 2.7 and 2.8—are designed to focus on mathematical thinking in a more structured context, one that is driven by curiosity. The initial actions, making estimates of a numerical quantity in a closed container, provide a setting for numerical analysis.

Task 2.7

Task summary: Analyze the numerical data generated when 11 (or another odd number of) children estimate the number of objects in closed containers.
Materials:

- Cardboard box large enough to contain 35 metal washers and with enough space so the washers will move around when the box is closed
- 2×3-inch sticky notes
- Chart paper
- Markers

Step 1—*Set up a group with an odd number of children (e.g., 11, 13, or 15) to estimate the number of items in a closed container.* The inclusion of an odd number of children allows for identifying the number in the middle (i.e., the median) of the list of estimates. Distribute sticky notes to each child. Display the closed cardboard box that contains 35 identical metal washers with a sample of the washer attached to the top of the box. Circulate the box, and ask each child to estimate the quantity and write it down on a sticky note without sharing the estimate with others. Some strategies that children might use to make estimates include evaluating the volume, size, and weight of the objects in the closed container, as well as the sound produced when shaking it.

After the children have had the opportunity to examine the box and write down their estimates, have them place their sticky notes on a large sheet of chart paper. Briefly discuss with them their reasons for their estimates. Validate their thinking about the properties of the objects and the size of the container (e.g., "So what you are saying is that you estimated 27 because there is only enough room for that many to still move around in the box. Am I right?").

Step 2—*Organize and analyze the numerical data.* Once all estimates have been posted, ask the children what they notice about the collection of estimates. As they talk about the differences, direct their attention to the numerical range in the unsorted list. Share with them your observations of the process of their search for the largest and smallest estimates. Raise the question, "How can we make this collection of estimates easier to examine?" If their ideas vary (e.g., lining up the estimates in ascending or descending order, or whether to make a horizontal or vertical list), encourage them to consider how the different formats affect the ease of reading the information.

Work with the children to organize the estimates. For example:

21, 27, 27, 27, 38, 43, 45, 45, 50, 50, 65

Engage them in studying the information and sharing what they notice about the numerical distance between each of the estimates. For example:

"Hey, two people agreed with me. It's gotta be 27."
"Wow, look at the difference between the lowest estimate of 21 and the highest, 65."

Validate the students' responses. For example: "So the difference between the lowest estimate and the highest estimate surprised you. Let's figure out what the numerical difference is in this list of estimates from 21 to 65." Have children share how they figured out the *range*. Continue to encourage them to look for more numerical relationships (e.g., "Which estimate is in the middle of the list?" "Is your estimate closer to the lowest estimate or the highest one?"). Use the term *median* when they talk about the number in the middle, and *mode* to refer to the most frequently picked estimate, where appropriate. With the children, record their observations about *range, median,* and *mode* for future reference.

Step 3—*Ask a child to count the washers in the container while the rest verify the accuracy of the count.* Have a child enter that number on the list and circle it.

After children satisfy their curiosity about how close their own estimate was to the actual number of washers in the box, make a table with them for closer examination of the pattern of estimates related to the actual number, as in table 2.3.

Table 2.3
Differences between estimates and actual numbers

Name	Number of Washers	Estimate	Difference	
			Estimate is greater than the number of washers	*Estimate is less than the number of washers*
Michael	35	38	3	
Natalia	35	27		8
Alex	35	50	15	
Amalya	35	43	8	
Eli	35	45	10	

As the children study the table, ask them what they notice (e.g., how three of the estimates missed by 8). Question how many estimates have a difference of less than 5 from the actual number and list them. Do the same for those between 5 and 10, and then again for those greater than 10. Ask the children to find the group in which their estimate fits.

Task 2.8

Task summary: Estimate with larger numbers.
Materials: Same as for task 2.7, except with a larger collection of metal washers, and some larger collections of other items.

Step 1—Repeat the same activity as in task 2.7, except for using 50 to 75 items in the same container. Follow the same procedure for recording and analyzing the data. After analyzing the differences in estimates from the actual number, ask the children to compare the findings to those from task 2.7 in terms of the range of estimates and the size of the groups when the estimates are arranged by numerical distance from the actual count.

Step 2—Use larger collections, up to 100, with a different set of identical items, such as metal balls or cotton balls. Follow the same procedure as above. Encourage the children to discuss the reasons for their estimates, such as, "I think there are two layers of cotton balls in this box and there are 25 on each layer, so my estimate is 50," or, "I don't think the container is big enough for there to be more than one layer of balls rolling around, so I think there could be 5 balls along this way [pointing to one side] and 7 this way [pointing to the other side], which means 35 balls."

DISCUSSION—*Tasks 2.7 and 2.8*

These two tasks engage students in fulfilling several of the standards in the CCSSM grade 2 domains of Number and Operations in Base 10, as well as Operations and Algebraic Thinking. In this set of curriculum activities, opportunities permeate to develop fluency with addition and subtraction within 100 (2.NBT 5). Through the analysis of the numerical relationships flowing from comparing small differences involving one- and two-digit numbers, students increase fluency in adding and subtracting within 20 using mental strategies (2.OA 2). Increasing the number of items increases the complexity of the task to involve two-digit numbers and computing using place-value notation (2.NBT 5). The task of grouping the estimates in terms of numerical distance from the actual number initiates thinking about fractions (e.g., the differences in more than half of the estimates were more than 10), laying the foundation for working with fractions in later grades. Through the overall process, children also engage in some of the Standards for Mathematical Practice by persevering in solving problems (MP.1) and attending to precision (MP.6).

Although the focus here is on mathematical thinking and problem solving, an application of scientific understandings about the properties of objects is critical to the task. For example, the science information collected on sounds produced when shaking the container is one consideration to be coordinated with the mathematics information of weight and size of the objects and the volume of the container in order to make an estimate.

Summary

The use of mathematical content related to CCSSM is integral to capturing children's interest in understanding the relationship between and within events in the tasks described in this chapter. In the kindergarten tasks, the context is one of a playful activity that resembles a game. In the integrated curriculum activities for grade 1, the project goal of creating a product sets the context for provoking children's interests. The context for the grade 2 activities is one in which curiosity is the driving force for thinking about mathematical relationships. As each of these sets of tasks for kindergarten to grade 2 increases in complexity, the focus on the mathematical actions shapes the progress of the activities.

It is important to note that the early childhood professional literature is rich with books and articles that describe curriculum activities that nurture children's ability to understand relationships within the base-ten number system and that begin to generate algorithms that can guide them in performing computations (Curcio and Schwartz 1997; Fosnot and Dolk 2001; Kamii 2000; Sheffield et al. 2002; Trafton and Thiessen 1999; Whitin and Wilde 1995). Although most of these resources precede the distribution of the CCSSM publication, analysis of activities in these resources can be effectively connected to the standards at the K–2 levels.

Chapter 3

Geometry

The study of geometry involves shape, size, position, direction and movement, and is descriptive of the physical world we live in. (Copley 2010, p. 99)

For young children, geometric learning flows from the organization of their discoveries about similarities and differences in the shape, location, and orientation of objects in their environment. It involves collecting and manipulating information about the properties of materials in their physical world, specifically the properties that define shape and positional relationships. In their daily experiences of observing and experimenting, we can see young children constantly sorting, grouping, and positioning the materials that are available. The toddler sorting pots and pans on the kitchen floor by placing lids in one group and the pots in another group is visually discriminating the differences and similarities in the shapes as well as the sizes. When this activity switches to placing the lids on top of the pots, often the action of *changing the orientation* of the lid also occurs. The preschooler playing with puzzles is concentrating on placing a puzzle piece into a given space based not only on its shape but also on the orientation of the shape. The primary-grade child drawing a picture in response to literature is using a variety of geometric shapes, figuring out where to position them to construct a desired picture that resembles a mental image.

A rich array of research studies over the past fifty years provide vivid evidence of the multiple ways children distinguish shapes in their environment, sort them, and construct with them (Clements 2009; Ginsburg, Inoue, and Seo 2008; Hirsch 1974; Wann, Dorn, and Liddle 1962). These reports reveal how children demonstrate their growing geometric shape and spatial sense in the early childhood years. When researchers looked at the frequency of different kinds of mathematical activity in four- and five-year-olds as they pursued their self-selected activities, they found that pattern and shape were the most dominant kinds of mathematical activity irrespective of income group (Seo and Ginsberg 2004).

The Dutch educators Pierre van Hiele and Dina van Hiele-Geldof formalized our emerging understandings of how *geometric reasoning* progresses sequentially from these early beginnings by identifying five levels or stages of development (van Hiele 1986). The first three levels— *visualization, analysis,* and *informal deduction*—fall within the scope of kindergarten through grade 2 of the Common Core State Standards for Mathematics (National Governors Association Center for Best Practices and Council of Chief State School Officers 2010) and are featured for further development in grades 3–6. The final two levels, *deduction* and *rigor*, develop much later.

The understandings reflected at the first level of the progression, *visualization,* include recognition of shapes based on how they look. At this stage, children match and group shapes based on their perceptual properties. However, they cannot specifically identify the properties of shapes. At the next level, *analysis,* children begin to identify distinguishing properties of shapes. Classification thinking is emerging but is still limited by perception. For example, children at this level can group different types of triangles, but they still view a square as a "diamond" when it is rotated 45 degrees (Clements 2004).

Sarama and Clements (2009) further detail how van Hiele levels take form in children's development of geometric thinking and give direction to planning activities that stimulate their thinking about how to solve problems. The five areas in which they define learning trajectories or paths from toddlerhood through age 8 are: (1) recognizing and comparing shapes, (2) composing and decomposing three-dimensional shapes, (3) composing and decomposing two-dimensional shapes, (4) spatial orientation, and (5) spatial visualization. These sequences in geometry learning provided by the researchers and theorists in the early-childhood field conform to CCSSM in kindergarten through grade 2, and they serve as a basis for the activities and teaching strategies suggested in this chapter.

The introduction to CCSSM states: "One hallmark of mathematical understanding is the ability to justify, in a way appropriate to the student's mathematical maturity, *why* a particular mathematical statement is true or where a mathematical rule comes from" (NGA Center and CCSSO 2010, p. 4). For young children, mathematical maturity in shape geometry is initially reflected in how they use materials when pursuing their own interests and in how they talk about what they are doing. Spatial sense shows up in their actions not only with materials but also in negotiating their surroundings. They cycle between discovering the shape properties of objects as they use them, and then using the discoveries to build generalizations that they apply to self-selected tasks and tasks posed by others. As children increase their ability to focus on events and relationships created by adults, the opportunity to pose problems that conform to their maturity and interests also increases.

The concept and skill development sequences suggested by van Hiele (1986) and Sarama and Clements (2009) are useful guides for designing instructional interactions and posing problems appropriate to progression through the levels of mathematical maturity in the early childhood years identified in CCSSM. For an overview of the standards for kindergarten through grade 5, see appendix 1 on pages 51–54.

The geometry standards for K–2 are partitioned into three clusters of standards. The two clusters for kindergarten are *identify and describe shapes* and *analyze, compare, create, and compose shapes.* The third cluster, for both grade 1 and grade 2, is *reason with shapes and their attributes.*

What follows in this chapter are tasks presented according to grade levels. Of the three tasks for kindergarten, two of them (tasks 3.1 and 3.2) support identifying and describing shapes in the context of discovering mathematical content. Task 3.3 supports analyzing, comparing, creating, and composing shapes in the context of constructing products using art and craft materials. For grades 1 and 2, tasks 3.4 through 3.6 support reasoning with shapes and their attributes in the context of playing games and constructing products using art and craft materials. Geometric terms and illustrations of the shapes discussed in this chapter are found in appendix 2 on pages 55–57.

The Standards for Mathematical Practice (MP), as listed on page vi, are woven throughout these domains. Depending on the problem, a subset of the relevant Standards is discussed.

Kindergarten

Instructional strategies for increasing the problem-solving capabilities of young children in *identifying and describing shapes* take form at two different levels of mathematical thinking. The first level occurs as a child discovers and validates the perceived mathematical relationships between and among objects, events, and ideas. The second level occurs when the child is solving problems by *analyzing, comparing, creating, and composing shapes* using mathematical understandings and skills in a high-interest task. Problem solving serves different purposes at these two levels. Task 3.1 contains a typical example of the adult support that can be provided in the context of discovering mathematical relationships.

Task 3.1

Task summary: Group three-dimensional shapes based on similarities.

This task sets the stage for multiple experiences of problem posing. Conversing with the child involves asking questions to extend his thinking about properties of two-dimensional shapes while using the proper labels of the shapes. These conversations support the child's ability to "analyze and compare" the unique attributes of standard two-dimensional shapes (NGA Center and CCSSO 2010, p. 12). If the child has acquired sufficient descriptive language to respond to an inquiry, the teacher can focus on eliciting an explanation of the child's actions. The following example illustrates this approach during a child's use of attribute blocks.

Teacher: "I see that you have separated these blocks into three groups, circular, rectangular, and triangular. I'm wondering why you grouped the blocks this way."

Followed by:

Teacher: "Let's take a look at these three different shapes—circular, rectangular, and triangular. How are they different and how they are the same?"

If the child does not yet have the language to answer these questions, then the teacher needs to provide the language in the form of a description of the adult observation of the child's actions.

Teacher:	"I noticed that you put the rectangular blocks in this group, the circular ones over here, and the triangular blocks over there. Let's check and make sure that this group doesn't have any circular or triangular blocks, just rectangular blocks." Repeat the checking procedure with each of the other two groups of shapes.

In each case, the purpose is to help the child make the current discovery learning accessible for subsequent problem solving. To do this, it is necessary to initiate conversation about observations of the child's actions to support growing awareness of the geometric relationships that are being discovered (Elkind 1999).

When a child is using mathematical understandings and skills in order to solve a problem, the effort draws on prior knowledge in order to make sense of the problem. The teacher's initial comments that conform to this learning level are designed to help the child clarify the problem that was reflected in the actions in order to persevere in finding a solution and to draw some conclusions (an example of utilizing MP.1). The next activity, task 3.2, is a beginning level of problem solving using three-dimensional blocks.

Task 3.2

Task summary: Make a construction using a miniature set of wooden blocks of standard shapes in different sizes.

This task is similar to the previous activity using three-dimensional materials to provoke problem posing. As illustrated above, the teacher's decision of entry depends upon the child's mastery of the properties of geometric shapes. An example follows.

Teacher:	*[initiates conversation]* "As I watched you placing the shapes together, I noticed that first you placed a rectangular block here. Then you put the block that looks like a ball on top. When it kept falling off you picked a triangular block and placed it on top and it didn't fall off. You then made two more constructions exactly like the first one and didn't even try to use the rounded block again. Instead you used the triangular block with a flat face. How come you decided not to use the rounded block in your constructions?"
Teacher:	*[concluding the conversation by summarizing]* "So what you are saying is that because the block that looked like a ball had a rounded surface, it just rolled, and the block that had a "face" that looked like a rectangle was flat and didn't roll. Am I right?"

The adult's description of the child's actions with the blocks began with using the language most familiar to the child, "ball," and subsequently introduced the more precise mathematical language of "rounded block." The question that focused on the child's thinking clarified the regularity in the child's repeated reasoning (i.e., MP.8). This supports the child's ability to "analyze and compare" the unique properties of standard three-dimensional shapes, and accurately name them (NGA Center and CCSSO 2010, p. 12).

Often, a child's spontaneous problem solving leads to additional opportunities to extend the problem-solving event. Task 3.3 evolved from a child's figuring out how to rotate a triangular prism so that its base rested on top of a rectangular prism.

Task 3.3

Task summary: Use the observation of a child's solution to a problem with blocks to extend problem solving.

In this task, the child finds a way to join two shapes to represent a real-world structure of which he had a mental image. For this child, the shape of the block did not change, only its orientation changed, which is a precursor to building an understanding of transformational geometry. An example of teacher-child interactions follows.

Teacher: "I was watching you when you first placed this part of the triangle-shaped block on the rectangle-shaped block like this and it fell." (See fig. 3.1.)

Fig. 3.1

Teacher: "Then you turned it on its side like this." (See fig. 3.2.)

Fig. 3.2

Teacher: "But then you decided to rotate it again so it stood on the side opposite the pointed angle." (See fig. 3.3.)

Fig. 3.3

Child: "Yeah. 'Cause that's the way I wanted it."

Teacher: "Was there a special reason you changed its position, turning it from resting on this longer side like this [see fig. 3.4] to the shorter side, like this [see fig. 3.5]?"

Fig. 3.4

Fig. 3.5

Child: "Yeah. I wanted this on the top" *[pointing to the top angle].* (See fig. 3.6.)

Fig. 3.6

Teacher: "Were you thinking of some building you saw that made you want this triangular block to look that way on your building?"

Child: "Yeah. Where my mommy goes to church."

Teacher: "So, you used the triangular block to make the top of your building look like a church. Does the top of the building you live in look the same?" (See fig. 3.6.)

Child: *[The child pauses for a bit and then answers.]* "No. It's flat on top."

Teacher: "If you were going to make a building to look like the one you live in, how would you do that?"

In this dialogue, the use of the child's familiar language served as a bridge to "correctly name shapes regardless of their orientations" (NGA Center and CCSSO 2010, p. 12). The teacher demonstrated the language meanings as she elicited the child's intent. Modeling "shapes in the world by building shapes" (NGA Center and CCSSO 2010, p. 12) was addressed by helping the child make a connection between concrete representations and mental images (i.e., abstractions).

For young kindergartners, the recommended entry point for problem posing occurs during children's self-selected and self-directed activity when it is possible to infer the kind of geometric thinking they are using in their actions (Casey et al. 2010; Chalufour and Worth 2004: Golbeck 2006; Schwartz and Copeland 2010). This practice provides the groundwork for posing additional problems that relate to their interests and challenge their geometric reasoning.

Grade 1

In terms of meeting the CCSSM, the focus of grade 1 takes on new dimensions as children are increasingly able to pursue interesting tasks posed by the teacher rather than depending primarily upon their own self-selected tasks. Also, they are more aware of what they know and have considerably more language competence to explain their ideas and understandings about shape and space. However, if we are to strengthen first graders' problem-solving capabilities in the more formal academic environment, it is still necessary to design tasks that not only conform to their developmental maturity but also to their interests.

In grade 1, the geometry standards involve *reasoning with shapes and their attributes,* building on kindergarten experiences of *identifying and describing shapes* and *analyzing, comparing, and composing shapes.* The grade 1 content requires thinking about part-whole relationships as a way to extend understanding about attributes of shapes. The two tasks presented in this section illustrate ways to use the context of games to involve children in solving problems that feature part-whole relationships.

Task 3.4

Task summary: Learn to play Level 1 of the "Fill-in-the-Shape" Game.
Materials:

- Game board with 6 shapes: 1 circle, 2 squared rectangles, 2 non-squared rectangles, and 1 triangle (see fig. 3.7)

- Game spinner (see fig. 3.8). To make the game spinner, add a spinner arrow on top of the circle, mounted to facilitate spinning, and have the pointed end of the spinner indicate the shape to be used for each turn.

This activity takes the form of a game, but it varies from the usual competitive format. In this design, children work with partners rather than independently, and there is no "winner" or "loser." The game ends when all the players have met the game goal, which is to exactly cover all of the shapes. In the follow-up discussion, the teacher has the opportunity to encourage children to share their thinking, expand their understanding of the relationship between parts to the whole, and keep a record of the different ways they completed the task.

The game pieces match the figures on the game board in size. For each shape, provide a few more pieces than will be needed to fill the shapes on the boards of the players. On the game board, the *triangle* game piece is congruent to both the triangle and ½ squared rectangle; the *small non-squared rectangle* is congruent to ¼ of the non-squared rectangle and ½ of the squared rectangle; and the *half circle* is congruent to ½ of the circle.

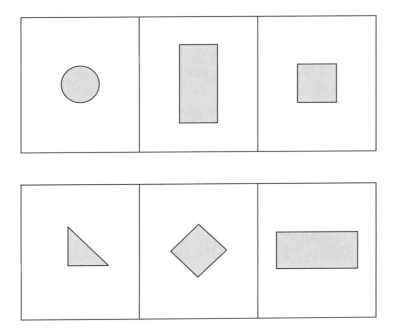

Fig. 3.7. Game board

Game Procedure: Children work with partners with each pair sharing a game board. Partners take turns using the spinner (see fig. 3.8). After choosing the shape indicated on the spinner, they decide where to place it as they work toward the game goal. The game is over when all players have covered the shapes on their board.

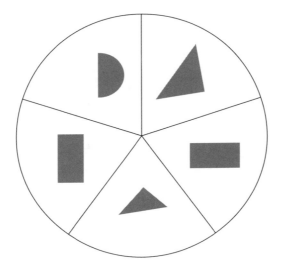

Fig. 3.8. Game spinner

Teacher Role: Explain the procedures while modeling the actions and supplying the language. For example, after taking a turn on the spinner, say, "The spinner points to a triangle. So now I need to pick up a triangle from the collection and decide which shape to cover. I could use it to cover the triangle like this, or I could use it to cover ½ of the squared rectangle, like this." As the first round of modeling continues, invite the children to think with you where you might place the next shape indicated on the spinner. If, as the game proceeds, a player cannot place the shape designated on the spinner, the next player continues with another spin. Repeat the modeling process if needed before leaving the students to play on their own. Remain with the group to observe the first round or two of play to be sure that they understand the game. At the end of the first game that children have played by themselves, invite the group to look at the different game boards and notice the ways in which they are the same and different in how the shapes were covered. Support the children's use of the terms *half, fourth,* and *quarter* in the conversation, reinforcing the notion that these labels make it easier for others to understand what they are explaining.

After completing the game, once again review with the players the different ways that they covered the shapes. Provide each team with a data collection form to record how the shapes on the playing board were covered during the game (see table 3.1). After playing the game a second time, repeat the recording procedure and compare the two events.

Table 3.1
Data collection sheet for the "Fill-in-the-Shape" Game

Names of Team Members			
Illustrate how you filled each shape during this game.			
Examples: **Circle:** 2 half circles **Squared rectangle:** 2 triangles			
Circle	Non-squared rectangle	Squared rectangle	Triangle

Task 3.4 addresses the CCSSM grade 1 geometry standard of describing part-whole relationships in familiar two-dimensional shapes (NGA Center and CCSSO 2010). The following task expands the range of shapes that the students will encounter.

Task 3.5

Task summary: Add a variety of shapes to play Level 2 of the "Fill-in-the-Shape Game."

As the children become more skilled in playing the game, invite them to add to the design, by changing or adding shapes, increasing the size of the game board and choices on the spinner. When new shapes are added, such as a hexagon or a non-squared parallelogram, engage the children in figuring out how many different shapes can be used to cover the new shape they are adding and which shapes they need to add to the spinner.

    With the addition of more figures, create another data-collecting table (following the same format as table 3.1) for the children to keep track of how many different ways the teams covered the new set of shapes (see table 3.2).

Table 3.2
Record of ways to cover other shapes

Names of Team Members _____ _____	
Hexagon	
Parallelogram	
(Other shapes)	

DISCUSSION—*Tasks 3.4 and 3.5*

The use of games specifically designed to focus on mathematical relationships creates the context for the players to invent more game possibilities that conform to the targeted mathematical content. The first challenge in this geometry game is to help children develop expertise in using their current understanding of the content to gain initial mastery. The game context is a high-interest format, and it engages the students in dealing with increased challenges and in keeping track of the mathematical relationships they have identified during the game activity.

The activity extends children's understanding about part-whole relationships as they use their language to describe equal parts of the shapes (NGA Center and CCSSO 2010). They are involved in making sense of problems as they figure out the part-whole relationships, persevering in solving them (MP.1), and attending to precision (MP.6) while using appropriate tools strategically (MP.5).

The increased fluency of students in grade 1 in partitioning two-dimensional shapes into halves and quarters provides the necessary foundation to focus on analyzing the attributes of three-dimensional shapes in grade 2. The kinds of tasks they can engage with involve a broader range of problem solving than that offered in the structured game format described for grade 1. Additionally, their social and physical maturity allows for greater independence and peer collaboration as they pursue the tasks in the following section.

Grade 2

The following set of activities for grade 2, task 3.6, is presented in two phases. It further extends *reasoning with shapes and their attributes* in the context of constructing products using art and craft materials.

Task 3.6

Task summary: Learn and practice the "Name That Block Game" for constructing three-dimensional figures using two-dimensional shapes.

This two-phase activity requires learners to identify two-dimensional shapes that can be used to construct three-dimensional shapes, using informal and formal language. The task increases the level of problem solving in an activity recommended in *Navigating through Geometry in Prekindergarten–Grade 2* (Findell et al. 2001) by extending the challenge from describing the properties of standard three-dimensional shapes to constructing the shapes.

Phase One—Identification of the unique properties of standard three-dimensional objects
Materials: Geoblocks and other three-dimensional objects such as blocks, cans, paperback books, cereal boxes, shoeboxes, cones, and tissue boxes.

1. Display each of the blocks and engage children in counting the number of vertices, faces, and edges for each block shape (see appendix 2).

2. Describe the face of one of the displayed objects, and ask children to identify the item with that face. Begin with the more familiar attributes of the number of faces and vertices as the primary clues before offering more complex clues such as "two differently shaped faces." If more than one object has the named attribute, keep adding clues to narrow the possibilities as needed. For example:

Geometry

Clue #1: "I am thinking of an object that has six faces."

Clue #2: "Not all of the faces are the same size."

Clue #3: "Four faces are the same size, and two are identical but are different in size from the other four."

For Clue #1, children might identify a cube-shaped Geoblock; for Clues #2 and #3, children might recognize a shoebox.

3. When children demonstrate a familiarity with language that describes the properties of the objects in the collection, shift the search to the objects in the classroom, beginning with the more easily identified objects.

Clue: "I see an object in this room that has two round faces."

Children might recognize these faces in a tomato juice can.

4. As children become proficient in finding the object with the described properties, ask them to take turns in describing a face of an object in the classroom for peers to find.

Phase Two—Engage children in figuring out how to construct three-dimensional objects using two-dimensional shapes and complete the task.
Materials: A collection of precut standard and non-standard geometrical shapes; colored paper to make additional shapes; scissors, tape, glue, ruler; and a collection of three-dimensional objects and photographs of three-dimensional shapes.

1. Introduce the task by discussing a plan to make a collection of three-dimensional shapes to place in a classroom geometry exhibit as a classroom museum in preparation for a special event such as open school week.

2. Brainstorm with the children about which shapes they can make and what materials they will need. Have the children work with partners and select the shape they plan to construct.

3. Before undertaking the construction task, ask each team to make a list of the two-dimensional shapes and how many of each they will need to construct the selected three-dimensional shape.

4. When differences of opinion occur between partners about which shapes they will need or how many of each shape will be needed, ask them to clarify their differences of opinion by figuring out which resources they can consult to resolve the question and what kind of information they can obtain from the different resources (e.g., a picture, a concrete model, or a written description). Encourage them to share what they found out and how they resolved their initial disagreements about the properties of the object they are constructing.

5. As the partners work on constructing their three-dimensional object, help them to clarify the problems they are solving as they make assembly decisions about

33

the orientation and position of the faces. Make observational comments about the way they are figuring out placement of the two-dimensional shapes, the positioning of the vertices of the triangles when constructing a pyramid, or the alignment of the sides of the rectangles used to make a rectangular prism. Raise questions about their expectations about how the parts will ultimately connect to form the three-dimensional shape.

Photo courtesy of Rosalia Frangatos

6. After the children have completed their constructions, invite them to display their products and initiate a conversation about their experience during the process. As children talk about their products, add the formal name of the shape to a child's label as needed. Present such information not as a correction, but rather as added clarity. For example, if a team calls its shape a pyramid with a square, add, "Yes. That's what we call a 'square pyramid.'"

    Next, ask the children to talk about which parts of the task were easier and which parts were harder. Seed the discussion by sharing an observation, such as one about how a child picked up a small triangle to align with a larger square, and, after testing out the congruency of length, exchanged it for a larger triangle. As children talk about their experiences related to the selection of types and sizes of shapes, and the challenges they met in assembling the product, continue to clarify with them the decisions that they were making as they solved problems. For example:

Child: "When we made the pyramid, we took four triangles. But we only needed three."

Teacher: "Were you thinking of a square pyramid instead of the triangular pyramid you wanted to make?"

DISCUSSION—*Task 3.6*

During this set of activities in task 3.6, the children engage in reasoning with shapes and their attributes. The task involves identifying various two- and three-dimensional shapes and then distinguishing them by their specified attributes (NGA Center and CCSSO, p. 20).

Students make use of several of the Standards for Mathematical Practice here. They are engaged in making sense of and persevering in solving geometry problems (MP.1). The task requires that they attend to precision in such actions as matching length of sides and forming angles (MP.6). As they work with partners, they engage in communicating viable arguments and critiquing the reasoning of their partner (MP.3). When they consult the available resources, they are using appropriate tools strategically (MP.5).

Summary

In this chapter, the suggestions for promoting problem solving that address the CCSSM for geometry K–2 involved three different approaches tailored to early-childhood developmental levels. For young kindergartners, the recommended entry point for problem posing occurred during the children's self-selected and self-directed activity when it was possible to infer the kind of geometric thinking they were using in their actions. This initial interaction serves as the basis for teacher decisions on how to increase opportunities for feeding children's interest in expanding their discoveries about shape and space relationships and in solving problems as they pursue interesting tasks.

In grade 1, the support takes on more recognizable teacher-planned activities with an emphasis on inserting problem-posing situations in those activities that capture and sustain children's interest as they figure out more about geometric relationships. With the involvement of children in expanding the game content by adding more challenges, higher-order problem solving increases. The recording of data offers an additional opportunity for strengthening and extending children's learning.

In grade 2, the focus is again on inserting or adding problem-posing situations to activities that are considered part of the curriculum. The kinds of problem solving embedded in the activity given here require children to share their thinking in making decisions and solving problems in order to construct a three-dimensional object using two-dimensional figures. The problem-posing questions primarily flow from the children themselves, and the feedback they get on the effectiveness of their decisions is related to the work they create.

At all three grade levels, the teacher serves as an agent for focusing children's attention on tasks, as a facilitator for clarifying the questions they are seeking to solve, and as a guide steering them toward ways to solve the problems on which they are working.

Chapter 4

Measurement and Data

Measurement refers to the process of determining the size of an object with respect to a chosen attribute (such as length, area, or volume) and a chosen unit of measure (such as an inch, a square foot, a gallon). (National Research Council 2009, p. 354)

As with all mathematical learning, concepts of measurement begin to build very early in the lives of children. In the process of manipulating materials for a variety of reasons, young preprimary children spontaneously make measurement comparisons. As they examine objects from many perspectives, children intuitively recognize that the objects vary in weight, size, and length. They will group objects based on one of the measurable attributes that most interest them at the moment (e.g., the larger cookies in one pile and the smaller ones in another pile). Later, we see them spontaneously placing a collection of objects in ascending or descending order (e.g., lining up the crayons based on length). Although not at a level of conscious awareness, this process of ordering a collection based on a measurable property alerts us to the fact that young children enter kindergarten with a considerable amount of informal measuring experience. The teacher's challenge is to help children transform this intuitive, informal knowledge into the formal knowledge needed for meeting the CCSSM standards through the grades.

The following generally accepted sequence in the development of measurement concepts and skills conforms with CCSSM for kindergarten through grade 2 in the area of measurement (Copley 2010).

1. Recognize that objects have measurable properties and know what is meant by terms referring to length, weight, and volume.
2. Make comparisons of measurable properties.
3. Determine appropriate unit and process for measurement.
4. Use standard units of measurement.
5. Create and use formulas to figure out the number of units.

The Common Core standards for K–grade 2 (National Governors Association Center for Best Practices and Council of Chief State School Officers 2010) in the area of measurement and data address all but the last level. The initial focus is on linear measurement in K–grade 1. Time is added at grade 1 and money at grade 2. The standards' sequence begins with describing and comparing measurable attributes, and grouping and counting based on identified attributes. The next level introduces the concepts of serial ordering and the use of identical units for measuring. The last level of this early childhood period addresses the use of standard measuring tools, estimating and verifying, comparing items, and representing the data. The following tasks are presented according to grade levels:

- For kindergarten, the first task (task 4.1) requires coordinating the attributes of length and circumference, based on both visual and tactile information. Task 4.2 engages children in using objects of different lengths to construct a length to match a single line and to then summarize the possibilities. The context for these tasks conforms with "engaging in playful activities and games," described as Context 3 in chapter 1 (page 3).

- Task 4.3, the first activity for grade 1, involves the measurement of time spans. It introduces the creation of a three-week calendar to serve as a tool for planning a curriculum event, a class trip. In task 4.4, children develop a daily schedule to inform participants of the sequence of the day's events during the trip. These activities conform with Context 2 (page 3) through "organizing ongoing activities and planning activity sequences for scheduling purposes."

- The grade 2 activities in task 4.5 involve children in figuring out how to measure the distance of a magnetic field and in choosing the appropriate tools for the task. The context for these activities conforms with "pursuing integrated curriculum activities" (in this case, science and mathematics), as in Context 6 on page 5.

The Standards for Mathematical Practice (MP) listed on page vi are woven throughout these domains as appropriate; the discussion for the tasks that follow mentions the particular standards that they engage.

Kindergarten

Seeing order relationships is critical to children's developing understanding of measurement (NCTM 2000). The measurable attributes of length and thickness continually absorb children's attention as they manipulate materials. In task 4.1, children establish equivalency in length or thickness of matched pairs of wooden dowels using visual and tactile information. The initial task of matching two identical items based on length focuses attention specifically on the alignment of the ends in order to establish congruence (thus meeting standard K.MD 2). Next, attention is directed to matching the same type of objects based on thickness. This task culminates in coordinating two variables to meet a specified criterion (K.MD 1). Task 4.2 strengthens the focus on congruency in linear measure by engaging the children in matching a single length with varying lengths, requiring an understanding of baseline in linear measure and the ability to count and record the number of objects used to match a given length (NGA Center and CCSSO 2010).

Task 4.1

Task summary: Match wooden dowels based on the attributes of length or circumference using visual and tactile senses.

Materials:

- 2 collections of paired sets of wooden dowels as follows:

  — 3 pairs of dowel sticks approximately 2, 4, and 6 inches long, identical in circumference

  — 3 pairs of dowel sticks varying in circumference, identical in length

- A shoebox with openings cut out at each end large enough for a child to place a hand inside each end in order to feel the properties of the objects that are contained (see fig. 4.1).

This task features the senses of sight and touch to increase awareness of the attributes of length and circumference (NGA Center and CCSSO 2010). The conversation during the task helps children bring their intuitive understandings to the conscious level and supports their ability to make sense of the problem and persevere in completing the task (MP.1).

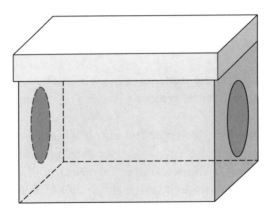

Fig. 4.1. Box for dowels

After displaying the matched pairs of dowel sticks varying in length and thickness, ask children what they notice about how the dowels are alike and how they are different. Ask them to demonstrate what they mean when they describe an attribute. For example, if the observation is "same," ask, "How are they the same?" If the observation is "same length," ask, "Will you please show us what you mean when you say they are the same length?"

First Level—Initiate the activity by placing one of each pair of dowels that differ only in length in the box and the other on the table in front of the children. Put one dowel in front of you and model the action of placing one hand in each end of the box, commenting, "I think that the dowel I have in my hand is the same length as this one in front of me." Take out the dowel, line it up on the table surface next to the one you pointed to and comment, "Yes, it is the same length," or "No, it is not the same length."

Invite a child to repeat your actions. Place both hands in the box, feel the object without looking inside, and take time to manipulate it. Ask, "Which one of these objects on the table do you think matches in length the one in the box that you have in your hands?" If the child seems to be searching in the box, ask, "What size dowel are you looking for—the longest, the shortest, or the middle-sized one?" Ask the child to verify the matching of lengths. If the child declares two dowels are the same length without aligning them, ask, "How do you know?" If the child puts the two together but does not establish the baseline, encourage the children at the table to help check that the two dowels are exactly the same length, that is, that neither end "sticks out." Share with the children what you noticed about how they checked for congruency in length (e.g., "I noticed that you took both dowels and stood them on end on the table to make sure they were the same length." Or, "I noticed you lined up both dowels against one hand and then put your other hand at the opposite end of the rods to check the lengths.") Return the dowel to the box and continue having children take turns.

After children succeed in matching the objects by length, repeat the process using the three sets of dowels of different circumference but the same length. Again, ask, "What are you looking for—one that is the fattest, the skinniest, or one in-between?" Once again, invite the child to check for the measurement match and encourage describing how the object is the same (e.g., "It is a round stick and it is the same length and same 'fatness'").

Extension—As a next step, have the students match objects based on one measurement variable irrespective of another measurement variable (e.g., match length but discount circumference).

In the box place one dowel of each pair from both sets (e.g., three that vary in length and three that vary in circumference and leave the others on the table). Ask the children to take turns finding an object in the box that is "bigger around or fatter" than the one you are holding in your hand. With each turn, ask the child to talk about how easy or difficult it was to find the matching dowel in the box and to explain why. Some sample questions follow:

"When your hands are in the box, what do you notice first, the length or the thickness?"

"Which measure is hardest to figure out when you can't see it?"

"When you are looking at this dowel here on the table, which measure do you notice first, length or thickness?"

Supply the word "circumference" as an additional word students can use when they are talking about "fat."

After children are familiar with the task, invite them to take turns choosing a dowel and directing a peer to find a dowel that varies on one attribute from the one that is displayed, either longer or shorter, fatter or not as fat.

Task 4.2

Task summary: Select dowels such that when lined up on the activity board they will exactly match the length of a 6-inch-long rectangular shape.
Materials:

- A collection of dowels of 1-inch, 2-inch, and 4-inch lengths with the same circumference, each labeled with a numeral for its length. (To avoid having the rolling objects, consider using lengths of Popsicle sticks cut to size.)
- Activity board for each set of partners with two 6-inch-long rectangular shapes
- Shoebox from task 4.1.

Model the task by selecting several dowels and placing them end on end along a 6-inch rectangular shape on an activity board to find out whether they touch each end of the space without gaps in between dowels (see fig. 4.2). Invite the children to try out the possibilities. Extend the task by placing all the dowels in a shoebox with ends cut out so children can retrieve the dowels before looking at them. Have children work with partners to retrieve four dowels from the box and decide which dowels to use in order to identically match the length of one of the 6-inch shapes on their activity board. They can return dowels to the box and retrieve a replacement as they choose.

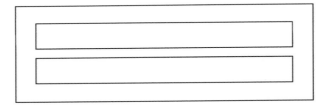

Fig. 4.2. Playing board

When a team returns a dowel or two to the box in order to make an exchange, probe their thinking. "What size are you looking for? How are you going to figure out how to pick the size you need from the ones in the box?"

After the partners successfully complete the task, initiate a discussion in which they compare the different sets of dowels they used to match the length of the shape.

"Did you always use the same number of dowels to match the length?"

"Are there two of the same-size dowels in any of these sets you used to match the length?"

Have the children draw a representation of their work or use precut shapes representing the lengths of the dowels to line up or paste on the chart.

Use a data-recording table similar to table 4.1 for the children to document by writing in the number of each dowel they used to fill a rectangular shape 6 inches long. After children have completed the task, set up small groups for them to compare their records of how they covered the 6-inch shape. Ask them what they noticed about how many dowels were used and the numbers on the dowels. Encourage them to add the numbers recorded in the table to verify that the lengths of the dowels add up to 6 inches for each shape.

Table 4.1
Recording chart for dowel activity

LINE 1	
LINE 2	

Repeat the activity, encouraging them to find different ways to cover the 6-inch shape and to keep a record of them. Again, have them compare with classmates, looking for which shapes are covered with the same set of numbered dowels and which are different. Invite them to make a list of the different ways the shapes were covered and count how many variations they found.

Extension—Increase the length of the rectangular shape to 8 or 10 inches, and repeat the activity including the recording and analysis of the data.

DISCUSSION—*Tasks 4.1 and 4.2*

These kindergarten tasks encompass a number of specific CCSSM standards. Within the Measurement and Data domain, they stimulate children to describe and compare measurable attributes of objects (K.MD 1) and compare two objects with a measurable attribute in common (K.MD 2). In the Counting and Cardinality domain, they employ counting to answer "how many" questions (K.CC 5). Related to the Operations and Algebraic Thinking domain, children will need to fluently add within 5 (K.OA 5) and to represent addition problems with numerals (K.OA 1).

Some of the Standards for Mathematical Practice also are incorporated here. In the first set of activities, the problems posed center on matching items based on an attribute, either identical to or different from the designated one. As they solve the problem of matching an object using only the touch sense with a visible one, the children engage in reasoning abstractly (MP.2). The second set of tasks involves figuring out ways to match the length of a rectangular shape using different lengths of dowels and documenting the results. The problem-solving challenge involves mental imaging of the length of the item needed to finish the task and finding it by touch rather than by sight. To persevere in solving the problem (MP.1), they need to understand congruency in length and also to attend to precision (MP.6).

Grade 1

Time recording tools serve a specific purpose in the lives of young children. They help them organize their expectations of forthcoming activities (e.g., "In five minutes we are going to have a visitor in the class to talk about the book fair next week"). They also help children make connections between the present and past activities (e.g., "Last week we started making plans for our school music performance and what we need to do to get ready. So let's take a look at what is first on our list and do that today") (Schwartz 2005). The tools can be used to support children in their ability to be active participants because they are informed about the sequence of events. The most effective way to understand the information about time sequences is to participate in developing the plan as it is being recorded. The grade 1 standards for measurement and data deal with the use of the clock as a tool to organize the scheduling of events.

The following activities for grade 1 deal with time measurement as it relates to planning a class trip. In task 4.3, a dedicated calendar format is introduced as a tool to organize the scheduling of events over a period of three weeks as a precursor to scheduling a day's events. It conforms with MP.5, "use appropriate tools strategically" (NGA Center and CCSSO 2010, p. 7).

Task 4.3

Task summary: Develop a schedule for completing preparations for a class trip.
Materials: Blank calendar form including 3 to 4 weeks, with days of the week listed but no dates (see table 4.2 for an example); chart paper and writing tools.

Table 4.2
Sample calendar

PLANNING OUR TRIP TO THE FARM						
Sunday	**Monday**	**Tuesday**	**Wednesday**	**Thursday**	**Friday**	**Saturday**
	Begin planning					
				FARM TRIP		

Prior to this activity, children should have had experience keeping a *weekly* calendar of important activities and events in their daily lives and reviewing them in order to plan for future events. Here, introduce the task of preparing for the class trip to a farm in three weeks.

Teacher: "After our discussion last week about visiting a farm, I was able to arrange it for three weeks from today. So now we need to start planning a *three-week*

43

calendar to help us get ready for the trip. First we need to make a list of the tasks that need to be completed."

Write their ideas on chart paper.

Teacher: "Now let's take a look at the list and figure out a schedule for taking care of all these jobs. Which tasks need to be done first? How much time do we need to get each task done? Then we can make a schedule."

Display the blank calendar and review the format with the children, noting the number of days in each week and the day labels. Enter the day of the scheduled trip (see table 4.2 for an example). With the children, review the list and ask them to begin to think about which jobs need the most time to complete. For example, they must obtain parental consent and recruit parent volunteers to help on the day of the trip. They must determine which jobs can only be done a day or two before the trip. For example, they must find out about the weather in order to plan which clothes to wear. As the planning discussion continues, encourage the children to be more precise and more detailed in establishing the schedule. For example, when they decide on the day to take parental consent forms home, ask about how many days should elapse before checking for the return of all of the forms. Review each item, assign tasks, and enter the information on the calendar.

After completing the planning schedule, check the calendar daily to monitor progress and add any additional items that the children think are needed.

Task 4.4

Task summary: Construct a clock-time schedule for the sequence of the activities on the day of the trip, using half-hour and hour time blocks.
Materials: Table for constructing a schedule of the day's activities marked off in half-hour intervals (see table 4.3 for an example); chart paper and writing tools.

Table 4.3
Schedule for trip

Clock Time	Activity
8:30	Meet at school with parents
9:00	Get on bus and leave
9:30	
10:00	

Several days prior to the trip, advise the children that it is important to inform the parent volunteers about the schedule of the day's events so they know what to expect. Refer to their daily class schedule as a model for helping people anticipate activity sequences and time slots. Brainstorm with the children about what kinds of information the parents need to know.

With them, review the list and begin to sequence the items along with clock-time specifications. For example, the bus leaves at 9:00 in the morning. What time do the parents need to arrive in order to be ready? Proceed through the list, focusing their attention on time and sequence by asking the questions "What will happen next?" and "How much time will it take?" After entering all the activities listed by the children, review the day's events in half-hour segments to verify that no important pieces of information have been omitted.

Once the schedule is completed, discuss with the children when is the best time to distribute the day's schedule to the parents and enter their decision on the planning calendar.

DISCUSSION—*Tasks 4.3 and 4.4*

This grade 1 set of activities, making lists and entering the items in a table, serves as an important precursor to understanding the process to "organize, represent, and interpret data" (CCSSI 2010, p. 16). The context for meeting the grade 1 measurement standard "tell and write time in hours and half-hours" (CCSSI 2010, p. 16) is established as children pursue a curriculum event of high interest for a purpose they understand. Discussions about how much time to allot for activities during a day increase awareness of the value of writing time using hour and half-hour intervals.

The children are involved in making sense of problems and persevering in solving them as they are called upon to think about the time intervals and make decisions in terms of what occurs during each successive time period (MP.1). The use of appropriate tools (MP.5) takes place as they move from the calendar to schedule events over weeks, to a daily schedule format to specify the sequence of activities over the period of one day.

Grade 2

As noted earlier, the most frequent use of measurement flows from children's curiosity about the properties of objects. The science question for the activity in this section comes from children's fascination with magnets and how they work. Task 4.5 has two parts, one focusing on the attracting force of different magnets, and the second on the holding power of different magnets. Focused investigation and the use of measurement tools and data recording not only feed children's curiosity but increase their understanding of the importance of attending to precision (MP.6) in figuring out answers to their questions. Because of the potential for multiple investigations, the following activities span several curriculum periods that integrate mathematics and science.

In the following activities, children utilize two measurement approaches, measurement of linear distance and measurement of weight, to answer a science question about determining the power of magnets. The two contexts for the tasks include pursuing integrated curriculum activities (Context 6) and satisfying curiosity (Context 5).

Task 4.5

Task summary: Measure the power of magnets, including their attracting force and holding power.

Materials:

Magnets: A variety of magnets in different shapes as follows, with written labels on each magnet to facilitate keeping records of the experiments (e.g., *Horseshoe magnet A, Horseshoe magnet B, Bar magnet A, Bar magnet B*)

- Different-size horseshoe-shaped magnets that vary in magnetic power to attract magnetic objects irrespective of size (e.g., a larger horseshoe magnet less powerful than a smaller one as well as one that is more powerful than a smaller one)
- Bar magnets varying in size and magnetic power irrespective of size
- 3 or 4 U-shaped magnets of the same size, varying in magnetic power
- Cylinder-shaped magnets of different sizes, varying in magnetic power irrespective of size

Magnetic materials: 3 collections of materials such as identical-size paper clips, thick metal washers, and metal cubes at least 1 inch in size, or a similar material that is heavy in contrast to the other two collections.

Measuring tools:

- Standard linear measure: Select metric or American standard units of measure based on the school curriculum:

  — Metric measure: centimeter cubes, decimeter rods, centimeter rulers and metric tape measures

  — American standard: inch cubes, inch rulers

- Nonstandard linear measure: rope, string, pipe cleaners
- Small digital scale
- Recording and marking tools: masking tape or other adhesive material, clipboards, paper, pencils, chalk, and crayons

Be sure to initiate this activity with children who have had prior experience discovering that magnetic force passes through space and other objects, and that people use that force to move objects in the environment.

Step 1—*Pose the problem.* Tell the students: "Look at this collection of magnets here. Suppose we wanted a magnet with a strong magnetic force to move a large object. How can we find how much force a magnet has? Which ones have more power? Which have less power?"

Step 2—*Encourage the children to brainstorm based on what they have already learned about magnetic force passing through space and attracting objects.* Provide sufficient time until children have no more ideas to offer. Record their ideas on a chart. For example:

> **Option 1:** "We could find out how close the magnet needs to be to pick up an object without really touching it."
>
> **Option 2:** "We could find out which magnets can pick up a really heavy object and which ones can't."
>
> **Option 3:** "We could find out the difference in the way two magnets attract objects when something is in the way."

Step 3—*Test the pulling power of magnets.* Suggest that all teams begin by working on the first option on the list above. Review the collection of magnets with them, pointing out that each magnet is labeled with a letter, as well as the magnetic objects provided for answering the question about the pulling or power of magnets to attract objects from a distance.

With the students, examine the measuring tools provided and recall prior experiences of using flexible tools, such as string and tape measures compared to using rigid materials such as inch cubes and wooden rulers. Encourage them to think about when it is easier to measure an object or distance with a rigid tool, a flexible tool, or multiples of unit materials like blocks.

Get them started with the following instructions: "With your partner, select two magnets that you think are different in their magnetic power. Following the first option above, test the strength of your magnets, using these objects. Remember that it is important to keep a record of what you did and what you found out so we can pool all the information when every team is finished."

As the partners select their magnets, ask them to share their thinking about why they think the two magnets they selected have different strengths. Observe the children's strategies and raise questions that can help them focus on figuring out how to answer the measurement question. For example, if partners are disagreeing about what the distance was between the magnet and the object when the magnet began to attract the object, raise the question of how they are going to mark the locations of both the object and the magnet at the point where the attractive force pulls the object to the magnet, and how they plan to measure it.

Step 4—*Record the results.* Talk with the children about the essential information that they need to record in order to make comparisons (e.g., the two magnets used in the test, the objects used to test the power of the magnet, and the results). Review the recording form with them, as in table 4.4.

Table 4.4

Comparing the power of magnets to attract across a space

Magnet type and letter label (fill in letter label)	Distance			
	Paper clip	Washer	Screw	Metal cube
Horseshoe magnet _____				
U-shaped magnet _____				
Cylinder-shaped magnet _____				
Bar magnet _____				

Step 5—*Evaluate the process and the results.* After the teams have completed their investigations, engage them in conversation in terms of three different areas of learning:

1. Measurement challenges,
2. Findings about the power of magnets, and
3. Increased knowledge about magnet power and how to test it.

Initiate discussion on these topics:

1. *Measuring challenges:* Invite the students to talk about the measurement challenges they faced in using the tools. For example:

   "When measuring the distance between the magnet and the object it could attract, which tool seemed to work the best?"

   "How did you mark the distance to be measured?"

   "Were you able to measure the exact number of units (inches or centimeters) or did you have to decide on the closest number?"

Enrich the conversation by sharing some of your observations concerning their selection of tools, changing the tools, and figuring out how to capture the measurement information they were seeking.

2. *Findings about the power of the magnets:* After discussing the way they solved the problems in marking and measuring distances, involve the children in studying the data. Focus on the measurement information by asking, "How do these data prove which magnets are the strongest?" and "Do you have enough information, or do you have to do more testing?"

3. *Increased knowledge about magnet power and how to test it:* Ask, "What surprised you about the power of these magnets?" "How did you think their power would compare before you started your investigation?" and "Did you realize how important the mathematics of measurement would be in investigating in science?"

Step 6—*Measure the holding power of the magnets.* Select the second option on the list above ("We could find out which magnets can pick up a really heavy object and which ones can't") to find out which objects in terms of weight magnets can pick up and hold.

Repeat the activity process followed in steps 3 through 5, having partners use the same magnets they used in the earlier activity. Have children keep a record of which objects their magnets (1) could pick up and hold, (2) could pick up and not hold, and (3) could not pick up at all. Using the digital scale, have the children find out the range of weight the magnet could pick up and the range of weight the magnet could not pick up. Pose the following question to the children: "I have a magnetic object here in my hand that you have not tested. If your magnet was not available, is there a way you could figure out whether the magnet could pick up this object?"

Once again, focus the closing discussions on the three areas described in step 5 above.

DISCUSSION—*Task 4.5*

This task incorporates several specific CCSSM standards as well as Standards for Mathematical Practice. In these activities, children engaged in measuring lengths and distances by selecting and using appropriate tools (MP.5) such as metric cubes, rods, or tapes to measure the distance between the magnet and the object when the magnetic force initially pulls the object toward the magnet. The measurement of a small distance and comparison of distances requires the same kind of measurement thinking as measuring and comparing the length of an object (2.MD 1, 4, and 9). In the process of analyzing their findings, they engaged in reasoning abstractly and quantitatively (MP.2).

Summary

Young children are perpetually measuring objects, distances, weights, and volume, often at the intuitive level. The activities described in this chapter illustrate ways to focus children's actions on measuring for a purpose that captures their interest and on sharing their measurement thinking with peers. The kindergarten activity narrows children's focus to measuring specific variables in a limited collection of materials. The appeal to think about the variables flows from the activity design that involves finding materials that are not visible to match materials that are visible. This "hidden to be revealed" formula generates high interest in young children; it was also used in the grade 2 estimating activity in chapter 2, which led to examining more complex mathematical relationships. Additional popular contexts for using measurement thinking to drive the actions are treasure hunts that require locating objects in the environment that have specified measurements, or are placed at specified distances; action games that involve length of movement of players or game materials; and musical-movement activities. The role of the teacher in each of these activities begins with shaping the focus on measurement and planning timely periods for discussing with children their measurement thinking as it took form in the actions.

Time and date measurements that can interest children require establishing a purpose for the activity. Calendar and clock reading take on meaning when the purpose is directly connected to what the children will be doing and when it affords them the information they need to anticipate and adapt to the forthcoming scheduled activities. The grade 1 tasks illustrate one of many types of events for which children can increase their time and date measurement skills and understandings by participating in the planning.

The grade 2 task, using measurement to accumulate information about a science event, illustrates the critical importance of using measuring tools to increase knowledge, not only in science but all curriculum areas. Discovering which tools to use in a given situation and how to use them expands children's options for further learning.

All of the tasks tap children's interests in ways that spur their use of mathematical practices and extend their understandings. As they seek to make sense of problems embedded in the activity processes and persevere in solving them, they increasingly engage in the mathematical practices that they can use over the long term in a variety of contexts.

Appendix 1

CCSS Overview for Mathematics in Kindergarten through Grade 5

Content / Grade Level	Counting and Cardinality	Operations and Algebraic Thinking	Number and Operations in Base Ten	Measurement and Data	Geometry
Kindergarten	• Know number names and the count sequence. • Count to tell the number of objects. • Compare numbers.	• Understand addition as putting together and adding to. • Understand subtraction as taking apart and taking from.	• Work with numbers 11–19 to gain foundations for place value.	• Describe and compare measurable attributes. • Classify objects and count the number of objects in categories.	• Identify and describe shapes. • Analyze, compare, create, and compose shapes.
Grade 1		• Represent and solve problems involving addition and subtraction. • Understand and apply the properties of operations and the relationship between addition and subtraction. • Add and subtract within 20. • Work with addition and subtraction equations.	• Extend the counting sequence. • Understand place value. • Use place-value understanding and the properties of operations to add and subtract.	• Measure lengths indirectly and by iterating length units. • Tell and write time. • Represent and interpret data.	• Reason with shapes and their attributes.
Grade 2		• Represent and solve problems involving addition and subtraction. • Add and subtract within 20. • Work with equal groups of objects to gain foundations for multiplication.	• Understand place value. • Use place-value understanding and the properties of operations to add and subtract.	• Measure and estimate lengths in standard units. • Relate addition and subtraction to length. • Work with time and money. • Represent and interpret data.	• Reason with shapes and their attributes.

Content / Grade Level	Operations and Algebraic Thinking	Number and Operations in Base Ten	Number and Operations—Fractions	Measurement and Data	Geometry
Grade 3	• Represent and solve problems involving multiplication and division. • Understand the properties of multiplication and the relationship between multiplication and division. • Multiply and divide within 100. • Solve problems involving the four operations, and identify and explain patterns in arithmetic.	• Use place-value understanding and the properties of operations to perform multi-digit arithmetic.	• Develop understanding of fractions as numbers.	• Represent and interpret data.	• Reason with shapes and their attributes.
Grade 4	• Use the four operations with whole numbers to solve problems. • Gain familiarity with factors and multiples. • Generate and analyze patterns.	• Generalize place-value understanding for multi-digit whole numbers. • Use place-value understanding and properties of operations to perform multi-digit arithmetic.	• Extend understanding of fraction equivalence and ordering. • Build fractions from unit fractions by applying and extending previous understanding of operations on whole numbers. • Understand decimal notation for fractions, and compare decimal fractions.	• Solve problems involving measurement and conversion of measurements from a larger unit to a smaller unit. • Represent and interpret data. • Geometric measurement: understand concepts of angle and measure angles.	• Draw and identify lines and angles, and classify shapes by properties of their lines and angles.

Content Grade Level	Operations and Algebraic Thinking	Number and Operations in Base Ten	Number and Operations—Fractions	Measurement and Data	Geometry
Grade 5	• Write and interpret numerical expressions. • Analyze patterns and relationships.	• Understand the place-value system. • Perform operations with multi-digit whole numbers and with decimals to the hundredths.	• Use equivalent fractions as a strategy to add and subtract fractions. • Apply and extend previous understandings of multiplication and division to multiply and divide fractions.	• Convert like measurement units within a given measurement system. • Represent and interpret data. • Geometric measurement: understand concepts of volume and relate volume to multiplication and to addition.	• Graph points on the coordinate plane to solve real-world and mathematical problems. • Classify two-dimensional figures into categories based on their properties.

Appendix 2

Attributes of Common Geometric Figures

2-D Shape		Shape Facts	
		Number of straight sides	*Number of vertices*
Circle		0	0
Triangle		3	3
Squared rectangle		4	4
Non-squared rectangle		4	4
Trapezoid		4	4
Pentagon		5	5
Hexagon		6	6
Octagon		8	8

Adapted from Findell et al. (2001, p. 24)

3-D Shape		Shape Facts			
		Number and shapes of faces	*Number of vertices*	*Number of faces*	*Number of edges*
Cube		6 squares	8	6	12
Non-cubic rectangular prism		6 rectangles	8	6	12
Triangular prism		2 triangles and 3 rectangles	6	5	9
Square pyramid		1 square and 4 triangles	5	5	8
Triangular pyramid		4 triangles	4	4	6
Cylinder		2 circles and 1 rounded surface	0	3	2 edges and 1 rounded surface

Adapted from Findell et al. (2001, p. 20)

References

Barnett, Vanessa, and Deborah Halls. "Wire Bicycles: A Journey with Galimoto." In *Emergent Curriculum in the Primary Classroom: Interpreting the Reggio Emilia Approach in Schools*, edited by Carol Anne Wien, pp. 52–63. New York: Teachers College Press, 2008.

Baroody, Arthur J. "The Developmental Bases for Early Childhood Number and Operations Standards." In *Engaging Young Children in Mathematics: Standards for Early Childhood Mathematics Education*, edited by Douglas H. Clements and Julie Sarama, pp. 173–205. Mahwah, N.J.: Lawrence Erlbaum Associates, 2004.

Casey, Beth M., Nicole Andrews, Holly Schindler, Joanne E. Kersh, Alexandra Samper, and Juanita Copley. "The Development of Spatial Skills through Intervention Involving Block- Building Activities." *Cognition and Instruction* 26 (2008): 269–309.

Chalufour, Ingrid, and Karen Worth. *Building Structures with Young Children*. St. Paul, Minn.: Redleaf Press, and Washington, D.C.: National Association for the Education of Young Children, 2004.

_____. *Discovering Nature with Young Children*. St. Paul, Minn.: Redleaf Press, 2003.

Charlesworth, Rosalind, and Karen K. Lind. *Math and Science for Young Children*, 6th ed. Belmont, Calif.: Wadsworth, 2010.

Clements, Douglas H. "Geometric and Spatial Thinking in Early Childhood Education." In *Engaging Young Children in Mathematics: Standards for Early Childhood Mathematics Education*, edited by Douglas H. Clements and Julie Sarama, pp. 267–99. Mahwah, N.J.: Lawrence Erlbaum Associates, 2004.

_____. "The Teaching-Learning Paths for Geometry, Spatial Thinking, and Measurement." In *Mathematics Learning in Early Childhood: Paths toward Excellence and Equity*, edited by Christopher T. Cross, Taniesha A. Woods, and Heidi Schweingruber, pp. 185–221. Washington, D.C.: Academic Press, 2009.

Clements, Douglas H., and Michelle Stephan. "Measurement in Pre–K to Grade 2 Mathematics." In *Engaging Young Children in Mathematics: Standards for Early Childhood Mathematics Education*, edited by Douglas H. Clements and Julie Sarama, pp. 299–320. Mahwah, N.J.: Lawrence Erlbaum Associates, 2004.

Copley, Juanita. *The Young Child and Mathematics*, 2nd ed. Washington, D.C.: National Association for the Education of Young Children, 2010.

Curcio, Frances R. *Developing Data-Graph Comprehension in Grades K through 8*, 3rd ed. Reston, Va.: National Council of Teachers of Mathematics, 2010.

Curcio, Frances R., and Sydney L. Schwartz. "What Does Algebraic Thinking 'Look Like' and 'Sound Like' with Preprimary Children?" *Teaching Children Mathematics* 3 (February 1997): 296–300.

Dacey, Linda, Mary Cavanagh, Carol R. Findell, Carole E. Greenes, Linda Jensen Sheffield, and Marian Small. *Navigating through Measurement in Prekindergarten–Grade 2*. Reston, Va.: National Council of Teachers of Mathematics, 2003.

Elkind, David. "Educating Young Children in Math, Science and Technology." In *Dialogue in Early Childhood Science, Mathematics and Technology Education, Project 2061*. Washington, D.C.: American Association for the Advancement of Science, 1999.

Eston, Rebeka, and Karen Economopoulos. *Pattern Trains and Hopscotch Paths*. White Plains, N.Y.: Dale Seymour Publications, 1998.

Findell, Carol R., Marian Small, Mary Cavanagh, Linda Dacey, Carole E. Greenes, and Linda Jenson Sheffield. *Navigating through Geometry in Prekindergarten–Grade 2.* Reston, Va.: National Council of Teachers of Mathematics, 2001.

Fosnot, Catherine Twomey, and Maarten Dolk. *Young Mathematicians at Work: Constructing Number Sense, Addition and Subtraction.* Portsmouth, N.H.: Heinemann, 2001.

Fromberg, Doris Pronin. *The All-Day Kindergarten and Pre-K Curriculum: A Dynamic Themes Approach.* New York: Routledge, 2012.

Ginsberg, Herbert P., Noriyuki Inoue, and Kyoung-Hye Seo. "Young Children Doing Mathematics." In *Mathematics in the Early Years*, edited by Juanita Copley, pp. 88–100. Reston, Va.: National Council of Teachers of Mathematics, 2008.

Golbeck, Susan L. "Developing Key Cognitive Skills." In *K Today: Teaching and Learning in the Kindergarten Year*, edited by Dominic F. Gullo, pp. 37–47. Washington, D.C.: National Association for the Education of Young Children, 2006.

Gordon, Alice Kaplan. *Games for Growth: Educational Games in the Classroom.* Chicago: Science Research Associates, Inc., 1972.

Helm, Judy Harris, and Lillian Katz. *Young Investigators: The Project Approach in the Early Years*, 2nd ed. New York: Teachers College Press, 2011.

Henderson, Kenneth B., and Robert E. Pingry. "Problem-solving in Mathematics." In *The Learning of Mathematics: Its Theory and* Practice, edited by Howard F. Fehr, pp. 228–70. Washington, D.C.: National Council of Teachers of Mathematics, 1953.

Hirsch, Elisabeth S., ed. *The Block Book.* Washington, D.C.: National Association for the Education of Young Children, 1974.

Johanning, Debra, William B. Weber, Christine Heidt, Marian Pearce, and Karen Horner. "The Polar Express to Early Algebraic Thinking." *Teaching Young Children Mathematics* 16 (December 2009–January 2010): 300–7.

Kamii, Constance, and Rheta DeVries. *Group Games in Early Education: Implications of Piaget's Theory.* Washington, D.C.: National Association for the Education of Young Children, 1980.

Kamii, Constance, with Leslie Baker Housman. *Young Children Reinvent Arithmetic*: Implications of Piaget's Theory, 2nd ed. New York: Teachers College Press, 2000.

Lesh, Richard, and Judith Zawojewski. "Problem Solving and Modeling." In *Second Handbook of Research on Mathematics Teaching and Learning,* edited by Frank K. Lester, Jr., pp. 763–804. Charlotte, N.C.: Information Age Publishing, and Reston, Va.: National Council of Teachers of Mathematics, 2007.

Lester, Frank K., and Paul E. Kehle. "From Problem Solving to Modeling: The Evolution of Thinking about Research on Complex Mathematical Activity." In *Beyond Constructivism*, edited by Richard Lesh and Helen M. Doerr, pp. 501–17. Mahwah, N.J.: Lawrence Erlbaum Associates, 2003.

Lowenfeld, Viktor. *Creative and Mental Growth*, 3rd ed. New York: Macmillan, 1958.

Martin, David Jenner. *Constructing Early Childhood Science.* Albany, N.Y.: Delmar, 2001.

Mitchell, Lucy Sprague. *Young Geographers.* New York: Bank Street College of Education, 2001.

National Council of Teachers of Mathematics (NCTM). *An Agenda for Action.* Reston, Va.: NCTM, 1980.

_____. Essential Understanding Series. Reston, Va.: NCTM, 2010–13.

_____. *Principles and Standards for School Mathematics.* Reston, Va.: NCTM, 2000.

_____. Reasoning and Sense Making Series. Reston, Va.: NCTM, 2010.

_____. *Making It Happen: A Guide to Interpreting and Implementing Common Core State Standards for Mathematics.* Reston, Va.: NCTM, 2011.